I SURVIVED POMPEII

I SURVIVED POMPEII

HILARIOUS ADVENTURES IN AN ELEMENTARY SCHOOL LIBRARY

RHONDA WILLFORD EBERST

I Survived Pompeii: Hilarious Adventures in an Elementary School Library

First Published in the USA in 2018 by Peacock Proud Press
ISBN 978-0-9981212-8-4 paperback
ISBN 978-0-9981212-9-1 eBook

Editors:

Laura L. Bush, Ph.D., PeacockProud.com
Wendy Ledger, VoType.com

Design:

Cover and Interior Layout: Melinda Tipton Martin, MartinPublishingServices.com
Cover Illustration: Jace Martin, MartinPublishingServices.com

Portrait Photographer:

Kelly Ortman, KOphotography12.weebly.com

Library of Congress Control Number: 2018937015

DISCLAIMER:

For Eleanor Lawton

Advanced Praise

Rhonda Eberst is witty, engaging, and a great storyteller. Be prepared to hurt from laughing so hard! Rhonda's dedication to children's learning and development is beyond compare. Every child needs a Mrs. Eberst in his or her life.

–Sonia Postema,
Parent and former Director of Human Resources,
Reynoldsburg City Schools

I Survived Pompeii is a delightful glimpse into the magical world of learning that Rhonda Eberst creates inside her elementary school library. With each vignette, Eberst celebrates the brutal honesty and powerful intellect of her young students, all while showcasing her own unique blend of self-deprecating humor, incisive social commentary, and pedagogical prowess. This wonderful book illustrates the myriad reasons that school libraries are unparalleled spaces for learning. It also demonstrates why school librarians must be extolled for the essential role they play in children's lives.

–Kerry Dixon, PhD,
College of Education and Human Ecology,
The Ohio State University

I Survived Pompeii is a must have for educators and anyone who loves children. Rhonda Eberst has written insightful and hilarious stories wrapped in words of wisdom and compassion. You will laugh until your sides ache and shed a few tears, too, while learning how to share your heart with children.

–Tammy Groezinger,
Elementary School Teacher

Rhonda Eberst finds true joy in working with kids. Through *I Survived Pompeii*, she reminds us to build genuine relationships with our students. Her ability to relate with students is a model for all educators as they embark on their own journey each day. Whether Mrs. Eberst is explaining how to solve the world crisis of kissing kindergartners or "line order," she uses her quick wit to connect with students. Rhonda's book reminds me of the pure bliss students bring to educators each day. Even when we want to cry, we can find the humor in any situation. I could not stop reading Rhonda's entertaining stories about her students. I found myself making countless connections to my own experiences. Her ability to find strength in herself and all her students is amazing.

–Anna Meyer,
Elementary School Principal

In today's fast paced, social media dominated world, it's easy to forget life's simple pleasures, like the joy of laughing at a story well told. *I Survived Pompeii* is a treasure trove of just such stories. For the last two decades, I have had the privilege of hearing Rhonda tell these stories to me directly. She is a master storyteller. The stories illustrate her sharp wit, her command of the written word, and her wonderful insight into the minds of the thousands of children she has worked with for more than 15 years as an elementary school librarian. Hilarious and often profoundly moving, the words and actions of her students will renew your faith and leave you with a smile.

–**James Coley,**
High School Teacher

"There is nothing
more contagious than the
laughter of young children;
it doesn't even have
to matter what they
are laughing about."

–Criss Jami

Table of Contents

Foreword

When Rhonda requested that I read the final draft of her book and consider writing a foreword, little did I know that I would read the book from cover to cover (twice!) on consecutive days. Sure, being a retired school administrator and professor makes such a feat more doable, but reading is one of many choices in my daily routine. Rhonda's book commanded my attention and gripped my soul for several reasons. First, she convinces me that personalized education matters. Rhonda's initial story about her own favorite teacher demonstrates how the daily words and actions of the adults in a school building can and *do* make a lifelong impact on the children they serve.

Second, after sharing her own childhood experiences, Rhonda weaves together a series of stories filled with caring confrontations and humorous incidents that entertain and inspire. Her collection of short stories make the case for changing children's lives for the better by knowing, trusting, empowering, connecting, and honoring students in our classrooms.

Third, Rhonda shows us how her library is much more than just a place for books and reading. She and her students transformed this space into a living library museum that supports both the school's theme and Rhonda's capacity to develop relationships. Rhonda believes that libraries should not always be quiet—that learning should be heard in active settings of play and discovery. She often credits her popularity with students to her zany use of hats or shoes that command children's attention. On the contrary, I contend that her special relationships with students, staff, and the community as well, extends from her top to her toes—and not just because of what she wears, but because her heartfelt efforts make students feel special each time they visit the library.

I recommend every educator read *I Survived Pompeii: Hilarious Adventures in an Elementary School Library*. These short stories illustrate multiple examples of relationship-building ideas that show any educator how to gain students' confidence and trust. Rhonda's book is not a step-by-step plan for improved student-teacher relationships. Instead, she reveals a symphony of beliefs and ideas for educators to consider as we personalize and improve our own practices.

Because Rhonda personally dares to be different, her stories challenge us all to reach out to children in newfound ways. In the end, she says that teachers exist "to plant seeds and nourish hopes and dreams for our students to have a wonderful life."

A wonderful life? Welcome to Rhonda's world.

–Dr. Dan Hoffman, February 2018

Dr. Dan Hoffman worked for forty-four years as a teacher, coach, and school administrator. He served on national boards of Phi Delta Kappa and the Coalition of Essential Schools. He was a founding team member of Metro High School, a STEM school choice for high school students in central Ohio, which is located on campus at The Ohio State

University. He was also a guest faculty member at OSU's School of Educational Policy and Leadership for over ten years. Dr. Hoffman is a recognized leader of school innovations and a frequent presenter in Ohio and beyond.

Acknowledgments

Recognizing all the people that made this book a reality is impossible. No one deserves more credit than my husband, Carl, who had to live with me through the process of laughing, then crying, then feeling like a total failure one minute and walking on air the next. And he thought my menopausal years were tough!

To our children: Leah, Liz, Katie, and Joe, who listened for years to my stories. I'm sure they will need therapy someday.

Wendy Helfan, who first suggested I write a book and offered help and encouragement.

Tammy Bish Groezinger, who took the original manuscript home and read it to her mother. Their laughter moved me forward.

Janet Benedict, who always believed this book was possible.

Dan Hoffman and Kerry Dixon, who showed me there are endless possibilities to being an educator.

Laura Bush, who helped me find my voice and gave me the courage to put it on paper.

Every teacher I ever had.

Every educator and administrator at Reynoldsburg City Schools who let me do my own thing and march to my own drum.

Finally, to all the children who walked through the doors of my classroom and felt like they were home. I adore them.

Thank you all.

Introduction

I am an elementary school librarian, which means I play for a living. Now don't get me wrong. I, like all librarians, work very hard. At the end of each day, I go home both physically and mentally exhausted. Although I don't have to give grades or worry about state testing, I do write lesson plans, run a library museum, and know the reading ranges of 500 plus students I see in the library at least once a week. Librarians like me claim full ownership of our classroom with its revolving door and endless patrons. My job is to champion books and reading skills. Equally important to me is encouraging kids and laughing both with and at them—something I know you'll join in with me as you read each chapter of this book.

School librarians, particularly elementary school librarians, are hired to "turn kids on to reading." As members of a team of extraordinary educators, we join classroom teachers and administrators in every educator's concern about scores and state testing. As librarians like me partner with other educators, we all engage the whole child. And just like any other educators, we librarians get to know our students, supporting them both academically and personally to help them become their best selves.

We also support teachers, administrators, parents, and mentors in their academic goals for each student. However, librarians do not have the daily pressures of multiple subjects and constant discipline issues. We know expectations for student achievement have never been higher for both students and classroom teachers. For that reason, Library, Physical Education, Music and Art provide important outlets and alternative success for students. Some students may not shine academically and struggle with the rigorous content of the curriculum we all now expect of them. When some students go to music or art class, for example, some may not be as strong as their classmates in core academic subjects, but by discovering their unique talents, they can shine in the choir or build confidence on the pottery wheel.

All students know who is considered smart and who isn't. They also know who is pulled out of the classroom for extra help and who isn't. Because of the expertise and partnership with classroom teachers, those of us who teach special courses can bring opportunities for all students to practice skills that build a struggling student's confidence and understanding that translates to his or her classroom success.

I happen to work in a STEM school where the curriculum focuses on design challenges and problem-based learning tasks. Our students transformed the library by designing and running it as a museum of vintage technology. It has become a place for research and development where students find books by genre and topics, Maker Spaces, and exploration. Libraries are no longer stacks filled with books, but areas called "Maker Spaces" where hands-on activities and learning take place. Libraries have reinvented themselves to allow patrons to research, discover, and explore beyond the written word alone. Partnered with books, Maker Spaces allow a much richer library experience for all patrons.

In our STEM school library, our Maker Space focuses on vintage technology and creative thinking opportunities. The library is also a fun place where students get to shine in their own way, and I get to teach in my own way—all while wearing Converse® tennis shoes and a chicken hat. To be exact, I have 32 pairs of Converse tennis shoes. Each day, much like Mr. Rogers putting on his sweater before he began his TV classroom, I pull on a pair of Chuck Taylors. The chicken hat is the first of many hats I purchased when I became a librarian. I wear hats when I read stories or feel the urge to be uniquely fashionable. Every year I even have my school picture taken while wearing the chicken hat to document how much the chicken has aged over time.

My hats and shoes are the result of being voted class clown when I was in high school. Growing up, I thought most things were funny and loved entertaining my peers. I was a performer. For Pep Assembly skits, if I wasn't borrowing Lily Tomlin's characters (Edith Ann or Ernestine, the telephone operator), I was walking around during the Christmas season with a wire attached to a headband and mistletoe dangling over my head. Once I borrowed a pair of Levi's from my teacher, Mr. Braginton. After filling the jeans with pillow stuffing, I ran through the auditorium as Bill Cosby's Fat Albert, becoming our football team's new secret weapon. I tell people that after graduating from Jackson Hole High School in Jackson, Wyoming (a small town near Yellowstone and Grand Teton National Parks that fills up with tourists looking for nightly entertainment), I graduated from the University of Dirty Jack's Wild West Theatre and Opera House. Most students like me run away with the circus. I chose to run down the street to the theatre. I refer to my years of summer stock theatre as the most important secondary education anyone can possibly experience. For ten glorious summers, I worked with and learned from very creative, funny people. My education covered a variety of topics, some of which were eyeopening for a sheltered small-town girl.

When I was a kid, my family never discussed the joys of liberal politics, religion (other than our own), or sex. Backstage at Dirty Jack's Wild West Theatre, these were nightly topics of debate. Sitting in the dressing room putting on my makeup, I tried to act sophisticated, all while making a mental note that I needed to do some research—and quick—so I could join in on the conversation rather than stare at my makeup mirror with my mouth wide open. As time went on, I grew to appreciate the mix of personalities and topics discussed. These discussions started to make me question whether I actually knew what I thought or believed about almost everything. I wanted to have my own opinions and be able to stand by them. Ten summers of higher education in the creative and humorous arts helped me to think for myself and become more open-minded, patient, and tolerant. Who knew ten years of summer theatre would prepare me for my life as an elementary school librarian?

Cultivate Laughter

Making others laugh and learning to find humor in most situations has served me well in my work and in my life. I always had a sense of humor, but when I was younger, I didn't always know when it was appropriate to be funny. During junior high, I expected my teachers to join my classmates in showing their appreciation for my hilarious sense of humor. Instead, I often found myself the recipient of an evil eye or a good scolding, especially by one teacher in particular, my 7th grade English teacher, Mrs. Lawton. Ultimately, she and her evil eye made a profound difference in my life, showing me that laughter is a great tool when used appropriately both in the classroom and in relationships. In fact, her guidance and concern for my welfare eventually led me to a career in education.

As clever as my humor was, Mrs. Lawton recognized that I used it like armor. I didn't feel like other kids. I was a chubby, crooked toothed girl who wasn't at all put together. I felt isolated. I didn't look like other kids. My home and family relationships weren't like other kids, so I believed I wasn't as valuable as my peers. I felt invisible unless I was making people laugh. I was sure everyone saw me as the reflection I saw in the mirror. At a time when boys and girls were trying to figure each other out, I never had a boyfriend. I was friends with everyone and always invited to all the parties, but when the lights went out and boys and girls would pair up, I was always left alone. I figured then I would be just a friend for the rest of my life. Mrs. Lawton knew that, even though I was surrounded by friends and was a leader who held a student body office, I was lonely, not because I didn't have a boyfriend, but because I lacked real relationships. I was a great listener to my friends but rarely exposed myself or my feelings to them. I didn't feel I had value. No matter how other people saw me, this was how I saw myself, and Mrs. Lawton knew it.

Mrs. Lawton was tough and matter-of-fact, with a bit of quirky thrown in. She had a necklace with nuts and bolts hanging on a chain. I liked the look and found her worth checking out. Others thought she was crazy and didn't understand her necklace. She had a reputation for being strict, a disciplinarian and scared a lot of students into good behavior. Many students thought she was mean and unapproachable. She was never going to be voted their favorite teacher. She rarely smiled and walked through the halls like a woman on a mission. She was strict and made sure students followed the rules. Mrs. Lawton was a bit of an enigma because the impression she gave didn't seem to fit with her necklace or her passion: the theatre. Although I wasn't completely sure how I felt about her, I did find her interesting.

In addition to her love for theatre, poetry, and American Indian culture, she had tremendous respect for the history of Jackson Hole, Wyoming, the area where I grew up. She gave her students a love for both, believing that every lesson in life could be found in Henry Wadsworth Longfellow's "The Song of Hiawatha." She even made us memorize a good portion to recite to our class. At the time of her death, another of her students, Ceci Clover, who had a column in a local newspaper wrote, "By being required to recite a portion of the poem, we learned mental agility and confidence in public speaking." Both were important to Mrs. Lawton and lifelong skills for her students.

Mrs. Lawton had an eye for knowing her kids and what we needed. If she wasn't the person to meet those needs, she found someone who could. She became a teacher who saw to our academic needs, but also one who looked after each of us as children with many needs and many dimensions. For example, Mrs. Lawton saw through my plan to use my brain only for things that were funny. One day she sat down next to me and said, "People care about you not just because you make them laugh." Her words stunned me. I thought I was doing a really good job keeping all my fears, insecurities, and secrets to myself. She went on to tell me that I had more to offer than what I was giving. She told me that she knew I didn't have the self-confidence that I wanted people to think I had.

"What are you talking about?" I said. "I have confidence. I am an actor!"

She didn't laugh. She didn't smile. She just looked at me. Her look said everything. I struggled to hold back the tears because she was right. I never told anyone how I felt. I liked being the class clown and worked very hard to gain the title because I thought that if anyone knew me for what I thought I was (fat, stupid, unimportant), no one could possibly like me. She went on to tell me that I was important to her and that I mattered.

No one had ever spoken so directly to me before. It wasn't just her words, it was the way she said them and the way she looked at me that changed my life. She spoke softly, quietly. She touched my hand. She looked at me without pity or judgment. She smiled. She knew how I saw myself, and she still smiled. That puzzled me. My secret wasn't a secret with her, and she still smiled at me. She became more than just a teacher to me. She became an actual person; she became human. Most students don't see their teachers as people. They are shocked to see their teachers or the librarian outside of school. They can hardly believe we actually shop at a grocery store or eat at a restaurant. I'm sure my students think I live in the library. Elementary students also see you as a nice teacher or a mean teacher. They either like you or they don't. I decided that day that I liked Mrs. Lawton.

It was then that I learned her quirky necklace of nuts and bolts had meaning. She told me it was time to get down to the nuts and bolts of learning. She told me that I was old enough to get down to the nuts and bolts of life. If she felt I was off track, she wouldn't say a word. Instead, she'd just shake those nuts and bolts as a reminder.

Because of Mrs. Lawton, I began to carry myself with a bit more confidence. I tried to listen to what people were saying instead of thinking about the next funny statement I could make. I tried to pay closer attention in class so my grades would improve. Though the changes in me were not always obvious to others, they were everything to me. Ironically, this transformation helped me develop my talent for being funny even more. I wasn't just being a silly kid with a sarcastic sense of humor. I was actually being funny. When Mrs. Lawton started laughing, I knew I was on the right track. If I was off track, she would shake her necklace of nuts and bolts and without saying a word, I clearly heard her message: "Get down to the nuts and bolts of learning." Then I began to notice I wasn't the only one she was shaking her necklace at. I wasn't the only recipient of Mrs. Lawton's care. Her message rang out loud and clear to those of us who knew what she was saying. With her help, I began to like myself a little bit more every day.

Be Real. Be Yourself. Be Human.

One day I questioned whether I truly mattered or not to Mrs. Lawton. She called on me to read the words reflected from the overhead projector to the chalkboard. I had to read from my seat in the back of the room. I had read for her before, but usually from a poem I had memorized or a script in a rehearsal. Instead, this was cold reading from a lesson Mrs. Lawton was teaching. When she called my name, I quickly slipped back into thinking "I'm not very smart." To top it off, I couldn't see very well from the back of the room. This was not going to be my finest performance. While trying to read, I squinted at the words and stumbled over sentences. Her frustration was growing as she corrected my mistakes. The more I read, the more uncomfortable I became, and the more I reminded myself that I couldn't read, and that I was, indeed, stupid. After listening to me stumble around with the words, Mrs. Lawton reached the end of her patience. She ordered me to sit down louder than I'm sure she meant to. Then she called on someone else to read.

I felt embarrassed and defeated. Sitting down at my desk, I couldn't look at my friends. They were uncomfortably looking at me out of the corner of their eyes. No one dared utter a word. They didn't know what to say. Then I did what only I could do to make the situation bearable: I hummed "Ding Dong the Witch is Dead" loud enough to be heard only by those around me. My friends chuckled under their breath. I felt better for a brief moment.

A few days later, Mrs. Lawton pulled me aside and told me she was sorry for embarrassing me. She told me she was having a difficult day. The tone of her voice and the way she looked at me exposed her as a human being. She wasn't just telling me she was sorry. She genuinely felt bad. This was the second time Mrs. Lawton said something to me in a way no other adult ever had. I don't remember what else she said or how I responded to her, but I do know that I felt relieved. I was glad she didn't say those harsh words to me because I was stupid; she'd just had a bad day. Though she was frustrated with me in class that day, I was important enough for her to apologize to me.

I have talked with many adults who remember things a teacher like Mrs. Lawton said to them while they were in school. Years later, they not only remember a teacher's words, but they can recite them with the same emotion they had when the teacher first spoke them. Sometimes the words were encouraging and helped the student grow; sometime the words were harsh or negative. Either way, what the teacher said stays with them. Whatever you say to your students, positive or negative, kind or harsh, they will remember.

I could tell you about some pretty remarkable educators that made a difference in my own life as a child when they showed me that I mattered. Mrs. Lawton was the most memorable teacher who took me, a lonely young girl, and showed me that through good times and bad, I mattered. She showed me that we all make mistakes and that's okay because everything can be fixed. Lessons can be learned. She was willing to say the hard things to help me grow, not only as a student, but also as a person. She was willing to be herself with me, showing me the value of being real with your students.

I didn't see Mrs. Lawton much through high school, although once in a while she would drop me a note congratulating me on a success. A few years after high school, I ran into her at the post office the day after her husband's funeral. I took her hand and told her how sorry I was about her loss. She was emotional and got a bit teary. Smiling, she said, "Thank you" and squeezed my hand. Neither one of us could say anything else. We didn't have to.

Several years passed, and I sent a wedding announcement to her from the Midwest, where I was pursuing my career as a school librarian. She returned a lovely card to me signed, "Mrs. Lawton." Then when my daughter was born, this same beloved teacher sent me a local newspaper with the date of Kate's birth to document what was happening in Wyoming on our big day in Ohio.

When I visited Wyoming shortly before she passed away, the impact she made in my life was clear. Eleanor Lawton welcomed me with love and affection. She hadn't forgotten me. She remembered things I had accomplished and things I had struggled with. I was important enough for her to remember. Eleanor gave me motherly advice about how to raise my children—the exact same advice she had given me long ago: love your children, believe in them no matter what they do, make sure they know how important they are, and when all else fails, laugh. The truth is I think I taught her that last piece of advice about the power of laughter. When it was time to go, I hugged my teacher goodbye, finally understanding the impact she made in my life. She didn't just tell me I was important to her. She didn't just tell me I mattered. She showed me what it felt like to be loved and respected.

As educators, this is what you can give a students: the knowledge that they are important as their own genuine selves. A teacher gave this self-knowledge to me, and I always strive to give it to my students. Mrs. Lawton wasn't just a great teacher who made a lonely student her project. She was an extraordinary woman who loved me and made me believe I truly mattered.

As a teacher, you and I are now taking Mrs. Lawton's place. Children will come and go from your classroom as they come and go from the library. You have the opportunity to influence, inspire, and love children. You don't have to put on a façade and always hold it all together. You get to be yourself. You don't have to know all the answers either. Teach your students with your specific personality and talents in the forefront. My ability to laugh and make others laugh has served me well. Find what drives you, what inspires you, what is unique to you. Are you a patient listener? Do you know how to make math fun? Have you got a knack for decorating your classroom so that it inspires and motivates kids? Those gifts will serve you well. Allow your students to know the genuine you by what you say and do. It's okay to make mistakes. It's okay to apologize. It's okay for them to see you sweat. By example, show each of them how to become their best self. When you do this, you will become an Eleanor Lawton or the teacher you remember that made a difference in your life.

A Parent First and a Librarian Second

My husband and I have four children. When our daughter Katie was getting ready to go to college, I remember a conversation around the dinner table. We talked about the educators who made a difference in her life. She was tossing around the thought of becoming a teacher. "If I do," she said, "I want to be like Mrs. Akers." Barb Akers was Katie's junior high social studies teacher who connected with our daughter. Mrs. Akers' lessons were engaging. She also had a toy Volkswagen Beetle and Bus on her bookshelf, telling her students, "I want to drive one of each!" That declaration alone was enough to ignite the dreams of my daughter, a soon-to-be driver. We also talked about Jackie Hasson, the first grade teacher to both Katie and our son, Joe. Mrs. Hasson taught with creative enthusiasm, insisting over and over that her students become good readers and writers. By cheering on their work and never criticizing, she built their belief that they had something important to say. She believed in them and they knew it. Mrs. Theaumont, their elementary school bus driver, drove them to school for five years. She knew their names. She found out their interests and talked to them about those interests on the bus. She liked them; they knew it. Even today, my children matter to Mrs. Theumont, and she matters to them.

Mrs. Potter, their kindergarten teacher could be stern and grandmotherly at the same time. Our son felt so comfortable with her that if he learned something on the playground that he felt we would think inappropriate, he would preface telling us about it with, "You know what Mrs. Potter taught us today?" One day while driving to an activity, our son said from the back seat, "Do you want to know what I learned from Mrs. Potter today?"

"Sure, Joe. What did you learn from Mrs. Potter today?"

"She taught us that if Katie had a girlfriend, she would be a lesbian."

My husband, Catholic-school educated and still feeling superior to products of the public school, tightened his hand on the steering wheel and told me under his breath, "Fix this." I looked at Joe in the back seat and said, "Joe, Mrs. Potter is correct. If Katie had a girlfriend, she would be a lesbian." My son was disappointed that he didn't get a rise from me and looked out the window, no doubt trying to decide what else he could blame on Mrs. Potter.

I could fill this book with names of educators and stories of my teachers as I grew up, as well as those from my children's experiences and especially my colleagues over the years. I am better at what I do because of all the educators who have crossed my path. The common denominator among each of them, however, is that the relationships they build with their students is their priority. Follow great teachers. Emulate them all while being your unique self. You will become a great educator when you follow the lead of great educators. How you interact with your students and your colleagues will influence not just the rest of your career but the rest of your life.

As you are building relationships, don't forget your students' parents. We live in a time where children bring the struggles of home with them to school. We live in a different world in education than our students' parents experienced. Expectations are higher, and there is more pressure to produce and be successful. When I was in kindergarten, we heard a story, had a snack, took a nap on a towel, and went home. It was a time when teachers were given the highest respect and rarely questioned. Today, opinions vary on the value of teaching. It is not the same gig today that it once was. It is vital that you know your parents. Find out how they felt about their teachers and school in general because their experiences will translate in how they deal with you. Your parents will be behind you, even if they don't always agree with your assessments, as long as they know their children matter to you, and you have their best interests in mind.

Educators Matter Too

No matter whether you're a teacher, paraprofessional, administrator, secretary, custodian, cook, bus driver, or school librarian, remember that you have been given charge of someone's child. Bus drivers don't just drive kids to school. They drive someone's child and your student. Their bus is their classroom, and their interactions with their students will help a child start the day. Cooks don't just feed children. They feed someone's child, your student. Secretaries don't just keep records, they know more about your students and their families than anyone. They don't just handle student information, they keep track of someone's child, your student. When everyone on your school's team knows their value and that they matter, then the students in your building will also know their value and that they matter. I believe that as an educator, regardless of your position, you can transform children's lives by showing children they matter. You do this by being your authentic self and building genuine, caring relationships with individual students in whatever position or role you play at school.

I love that elementary school is the time for children to test the waters—figure out how to maneuver through the challenges of learning. It's a time for children to make new friends, not just with other children, but with adults outside their family. It's a time for them to learn how to think, to discover who they are, and what they can be. It's a time to make mistakes and know that someone will help them and love them through the process of fixing those mistakes. It's a time to begin to write the rough draft of their lives. If you can give your students this foundation from the start, then you can turn them over to middle school, junior high, and high school teachers to do what they do best: guide and support young people to becoming outstanding adults. Your students, our students, our kids, will then write a phenomenal life story co-authored by you, their teacher.

If you're lucky, your students may remember a handful of engaging lessons you taught, but most likely, they will remember how you treated them, how you laughed with them, and how you cried with them. They will remember how you made them feel about themselves. One thing you want your students to take with them when they leave your classroom is knowing without a doubt that they mattered to you.

In this gig, you will spend sleepless nights worrying about your students. You will spend countless dollars, buying supplies and materials you need to create engaging lessons for your students. You will buy more Girl Scout cookies than you think you can consume. (Trust me, during testing week, you'll consume them.) You will create 25 different lesson plans for one concept because you know you have 25 individuals you need to reach. You will spend countless hours outside of the classroom building relationships by attending church plays, sports events, and piano recitals. From personal experience, you might even be called a Rock Star if you shout out a student's name and start the wave at their community basketball game. Showing kids that they matter gets families talking about you around the dinner table because they remember what you did for them. They know that you matter too.

I wrote this book because children matter to me. The work I do and the school district I work for matter to me. The people I work with matter to me. Building genuine, lifelong relationships matter to me. My kids make me laugh. They also drive me crazy. At the end of a day, I'm often left speechless and exhausted, but through it all, they make me laugh. And in the words of a first grader, "They make my heart sing." Because of them, I have the best job in education. When you let kids be funny and innocently honest, they discover they are unique and that their authentic self is a grand adventure to be discovered. In many instances, I have changed the names of the children in these adventures, but they are all based on my real-life conversations with kids.

I love the children in the stories that follow. I hope you will fall in love with them too. I also hope all my students will continue their innocent, funny, sometimes inappropriate responses to learning and life throughout their lifetime.

Oh, and I secretly hope at least one of them gets voted Class Clown.

I Survived Pompeii

When it comes to reading fiction, Tommy, a second grader, struggles. He keeps his struggle a secret from his peers by carrying around books like *War and Peace* or *Lord of the Rings*, sending the message that he is a reader. Tommy's serious expressions and details of Frodo and the ring make other second graders see him as their reading hero. They look at Tommy with respect when he shares detailed scenes from the movie *Lord of the Rings*, all while holding an unopened book.

When it comes to nonfiction, however, Tommy's demeanor changes. He no longer puts on the façade of a literary intellectual. He lets you see him as a second-grade boy genuinely excited about volcanoes. His eyes light up and his cheeks grow rosy as he excitedly brings a copy of a book about Mount Vesuvius and Pompeii to my desk.

"You found one of my favorite books," I say.

"I love volcanoes! They're cool," he says.

"I've been to Pompeii," I tell him.

He looks up at me, rather impressed. "Wow!"

I open the book and show him a drawing of Pompeii. In the drawing, the city sits at the base of the exploding mountain with lava shooting into the sky, dramatically flowing downward, devouring everything below. Placing my finger on the picture of Pompeii, I say, "This is the city of Pompeii. I was there!"

He stares at the picture in silence. Then, with his eyes wide and his mouth falling open, Tommy slowly looks up at me in awe and says, "I'm so glad you survived!"

1

Adventures in Surviving the Gig

There are days with kids at school when you are sure you won't survive until Winter Break. The truth is you aren't even sure you'll survive to the end of the day. It begins with a real Ghostbuster moment when you kneel down on the floor to help a student with her reading. One look at her and you realize it's cold and flu season; before you can get up off the floor, she looks at you with her glazed eyes and red nose, and you're slimed.

Next thing you know, you trip and fall. While lying on the floor, a group of students surround you with questions about library books, assignments, their need to borrow a pencil, or why they can't log on to the computer. They patiently wait for the answer as though your position on the carpet is an everyday occurrence. Finally, someone smiles at you and asks, "Are you okay down there?"

After spending forty-five minutes with children bouncing off the walls, you wish you were lying on the floor behind your desk so no one can find you. Just as you're about to pick up the phone and call the retirement system, a first grader with tears in his eyes apologize for going bonkers. You accept the apology just in time because you are about to go bonkers yourself.

In other words, I understand how real life affects our interactions with our students and colleagues. There's a little word women of my age use called "menopause," and when I am having those moments where I am testy because of my changing life or preoccupied with other adult stresses, I often think back to the day I read out loud in my 7th grade English class. I've tried to make it a point to be real with my students, make myself relatable, and do everything in my power to show them they matter, even when my responses are interpreted otherwise.

One day, Toby, a second grader, forgot his library book. Again. It had been several weeks, and I wasn't in the mood for another lost book. Nor was I in the mood for his disruptive behavior. I came to school testy, spent most of the day testy, and by the last period of the day when Toby's class came, my menopausal meltdown was ready to surface. When he told me he couldn't find his book again, I lost all perspective. I didn't yell, but my body language and the tone of my voice made Toby cry. The whole class gasped. My words were pointed and strained. No one doubted Mrs. Eberst was upset. During another interaction with a third grader that same week, she told me I was a little "yelly," so I quickly corrected my response to her. With Toby, though, I was incapable of self-correction.

After repeating my frustrations in every way that I could possibly express with Toby, I pointed to the table and demanded that he sit down and find something to read! The class was quiet and started reading their books without incident. I was aware of the concerned looks on their faces and the quiet tears Toby was shedding while trying to read his own book. Just as my real self who loves her students wanted to surface and put my arms around this child, my evil menopausal twin was too strong to resist and would look at the clock willing the day to be over, all while scowling, drooling, and letting my head turn in circles.

When I got home that night, I started feeling remorse. I couldn't believe I made Toby cry. He was just a little boy who had more struggles in his life than most second graders. The hardest part was knowing that he liked me, and I couldn't stand how I had made him feel. As a kid, I had been on the receiving end of such a disdainful tone on more than one occasion, and I knew how I had felt. That night, I didn't sleep, feeling pained at how I had hurt Toby. The following morning when I walked outside to go to school, this feeling of guilt ate away at me. I felt so bad, I looked up to make sure a house wasn't about to fall on my head. I wore my red-and-white-striped socks and ruby Converse shoes, just in case.

After the morning bell rang, I went to Toby's class and called him out to the hall. The look on his face when he saw me told me exactly what he was thinking: "What does she want? I don't have my book. I don't care about the stupid book. Leave me alone!" Instead of standing and looking down on him as I had done the day before, I got on my knees so I could look him directly in the eyes. As I took Toby's hands in mine, he stiffened and looked down at the floor. Speaking slowly and calmly, I did my best not to cry. "I wasn't very nice to you yesterday. I was having a really bad day, and I took it out on you. I'm sorry. Toby, you are more important to me than a library book. I made you feel like a book meant more to me than you do. That's just not true. You matter more to me than a book. If you can't find it, we will figure it out together. I'm sorry Toby. Please forgive me."

When he looked up at me, he had tears in his eyes. Without saying a word, he threw his arms tightly around my neck, then ran back to his class. I walked back to the library and cried. From that day on, when I saw Toby in the halls, he didn't avoid eye contact.

He would give me a little smile and a quick wave. A few days after I asked Toby to forgive me, he ran into the library with a book in hand, shouting that he had found his library book. We celebrated with a high five and big smiles. I asked him how he found it. "I looked for it for the first time last night!" At that moment, I knew he had never heard anything I said to him those days in the library when I was nagging him about bringing his book back. He had just tuned me out. After proving to him that he mattered to me, he became a different little boy.

You know what I'm talking about when it comes to moments like these—both the highs and lows of interacting with your students. Sometimes you fail; sometimes you succeed. As an educator, you face the challenges and the successes daily. Then, after making it through the end of each and every day, you wake up the next morning to find twenty-five years have passed. Not only have you survived schedules, duties, testing and never-ending moments where you shook your head and looked dumbfounded at what you've seen and heard, you've made it through the most challenging of times. In fact, you think you never want to experience it again. Eventually, though, you realize that you not only survived the gig, you thrived. Twenty-five years of students thrived right along with you, and the moments you thought you would never get through were the moments that helped shape the last two decades—not just for you, but for the children who walked through the doors of your classroom.

Right now, it might feel like you're just surviving the teaching gig, especially if this is your first year. But in truth, it's the most challenging moments that help both you and your students be the best that you can be. These moments make the best memories. They're the best stories to share with your friends, and who knows, maybe someday, you'll write a book!

Ready for the School Year

- ✓ Converse chosen
- ✓ Class list on desk
- ✓ Read-a-loud selected
- ✓ Schedule set
- ✓ Flask in purse

Please Open the Door

The sun is deceptive, as I walk outside at the end of the day to see which of the buses has arrived. It has been a week of sub-zero temperatures, yet the sky is blue and the sun is bright.

As I turn to go back inside the building, the blue sky and brilliant sun reflect off the glass doors. I put my face close to the glass, and with my foggy eyeglasses, I'm thrilled to see someone on the other side. This means I don't have to take off my gloves and unzip my coat to find my key to the building.

I tap on the glass, smile and say, "Please open the door." I have to knock and shout louder to get the attention of the person looking back at me. We teach our students not to open the door to the outside for anyone, but surely they recognize me even in the arctic tundra coat and the fogged glasses I'm wearing. I knock again. Again, I'm ignored and soon grow impatient.

I knock louder and repeat my request slowly and clearly. "Please. Open. The. Door." It doesn't take long after my direct plea to realize the person looking back at me, making no attempt to open the door to let me in from the cold, is my own reflection.

Beauty Parlor

I love morning bus duty. It gives me a chance to see the kids as they get off the bus and welcome them to the new school day. Once in a while, I'm called to a bus by one of the drivers needing help. I can usually tell by the driver's expression if we have a serious issue and if I'm going to need backup. This time, with radio in hand and ready to press the help button, I board the bus. I'm not sure what I'm facing by the driver's expression. It isn't one I recognize. I'm a little nervous, as this is a seasoned driver who has seen it all. He doesn't say a word—just points down the long aisle to the back of the bus. I can't see anything until I come directly upon the students. The high seats block the tiny three-foot-tall boys. When they come into view, I know why the driver has the expression on his face that he does.

In front of me sit two second grade boys who have decided to play beauty parlor on their way to school with the hair gel one took from his sister's room. They are both covered in florescent pink gel. There is hair matted down with thick ooze, and their hands are coated in dried crusty pink. The gel is all over their coats, book bags, seat, and the walls of the bus. I don't know what to say. I look down at them, and they look up at me. No one speaks except the bus driver who is now standing next to me reminding me that it's only six days until winter break.

So Do I, Kid

It doesn't happen very often, but once in a while I just can't take it anymore. Kindergarten. What more can I say? I reach a point where I'm not very sympathetic to the nonstop ills of five-year-old children.

"My leg hurts," Mary whines.

"So does mine," I say.

"I have a headache, Mrs. Eberst."

"Ya? Well, so do I."

"I don't feel good."

"Neither do I!"

"My finger hurts."

"Welcome to the club!"

"I have pretty shoes," says Sarah, holding up her leg to show me.

"So do I," I say, picking up my foot so she can see mine.

"I want to go home," says Timmy.

"So do I, kid. So do I."

Nothing Better. Nothing Worse.

Five-year-olds can fill your heart with joy, confirming why you went in to education. In fact, there's nothing better than getting a big hug from a kindergartner. These tiny people can make you feel good about yourself when they smile and say, "You're pretty." But five-year-olds can also rip your heart out, send you into a tailspin of despair and force you to relive your chubby, insecure middle school years. There's nothing worse, for example, than having a kindergartner reach down and pat your stomach while hugging you tightly with endless affection, asking if you have a baby in your belly.

Flu Season

✓ One: Very sick student throwing up on the bus.
✓ One: Principal.
✓ One: Librarian (me) on bus duty.
✓ Two: Pair of rubber gloves.
✓ One: Large roll of paper towels.
✓ One: Giant trash bag.
✓ One: Librarian job description that reads, "All other duties so assigned."

Note to Self

When reading the picture book *EIEIO: How Old MacDonald Got His Farm (with A Little Help from a Hen)* by Judy Sierra to a group of first graders, I learn it's a good idea when explaining COMPOST, to use the word "manure" or "fertilizer" in place of reading the word POOP.

In other words, if you want six-year-olds to understand the concept of composting, do not say, read, or even insinuate the word POOP. They'll be too busy giggling and shouting out the word POOP to remember anything else you read to them.

Santa is Coming Soon

I didn't need the weatherman to tell me a storm is coming or that winter break is just around the corner. I have kindergartners in the library. There is something in the air today. I can feel it when I walk into the room. The message eerily floats in like the green fog angel of death in the 1956 movie *The Ten Commandments*. The message is clear: No matter how good I think I am with children, I don't have a chance today.

It begins with Arlene dancing her way into the room singing, "Books. Books. Books. I love books." She keeps singing while Jimmy tattles on Brittany and says she hit him with her library stick.

Connie Jo, dressed for the holiday, looks up at me and says sweetly, "Santa is coming soon."

Before I can respond to Connie Jo, Jimmy finds another person to tattle on and shouts, "Mrs. Eberst, Donald is picking his nose!"

"Don't pick your nose!" I sternly tell Donald. "Get a tissue from my desk."

As soon as I turn my back, a group of girls cries out, "Eeeeewwww. He ate his booger!"

"Don't eat your booger! Get a tissue. Then go wash your hands!" I glance at the clock, hoping class is over, but only a few minutes have ticked by since the green fog entered the room.

Feeling a tug, I look down and there stands Connie Jo. With the same sweet smile, she again shares the news that "Santa is coming soon!" Once again, I ignore her when I hear screams coming from the other side of the room. By a pile of books that moments ago were in perfect order on the shelf, Tom is on the floor, flat on his back. He's holding a book in each hand, insisting, "I didn't do it! I didn't do it!" Other students begin rushing toward the pile like shoppers on Black Friday, as Arlene is twirling around shouting, "Ugly Alert! Ugly Alert!" This is exactly what I say when students have messed up the bookshelves and aren't being responsible with their shelf markers. At that moment, I curse myself for teaching 25 kindergartners "the ugly shelf alert."

Jimmy has made his way to my desk and shouts to me that Donald is now trying to get him to eat his boogers. I rush to the circulation desk, "No. No. No. No. Get a tissue!" As I hand the box of Kleenex to Donald, Ann yells out that she has to go to the bathroom.

"Go!" I shout back. Ann squats down and goes to the bathroom.

"Mrs. Eberst, Ann urinated on the floor!" Lorraine tells me. Not sure I've heard her correctly I ask, "What?" Lorraine thinks I don't know the definition of urinate, so she shouts at the top of her lungs. "Ann peed on the floor!" I look over to see Ann standing in a wet puddle in the middle of the picture book stacks. "Go to the office and get cleaned up," I order.

Connie Jo has now morphed into Dr. Seuss's Cindy Loo Who, trying to be heard above the commotion and shouting, "Santa is coming soon! Santa is coming soon!" Arlene continues to lead a group of students dancing around books still on the floor as she shouts, "Ugly Alert. Ugly Alert!"

Yes. Things are getting ugly. How did I lose control so quickly? I raise my hands and give the code for everyone to be quiet. "Spark!" I shout. "Go to the reading corner. Everyone. Now!"

Twenty-five five-year-olds happily skip to the reading corner. As soon as we sit on the floor, I hear Jimmy say, "EEEWWWW! Billy farted!"

Determined to take back control, I tell him that everyone farts. It is a natural bodily function. Ignore it! Before I finish speaking, I catch the scent of Billy's fart. I have never smelled anything like it. I had no idea a human being, let alone a child, could produce such an offensive odor. All the students, including the farter, are holding their noses. My eyes start to water, and every last breath leaves my body. Trying to breathe through my mouth, I sound like a munchkin as I call out directions. "Go, go to the front of the library! Now!"

Students holding their noses ignore the rule of NO RUNNING and dash to the front of the room. I want to make a mad dash myself when two students grab my hands. "Oh, good Lord! It's the picker and the farter," I think to myself, eyes still watering. Letting go of their hands, I tell them to "Run. Run like the wind to the front of the library." Off they run.

My head is spinning. I channel the spirit of Charlton Heston starring in *Planet of the Apes*. Falling to my knees, I pound my fists on the carpet and shout: "It's a mad house! A MAD HOUSE!" I watch my students as they dance in slow motion around the library hearing their muffled cries of "Ugly Alert! Ugly Alert!" They sing as they hold their shelf markers toward the sky, dancing as if in pagan ritual.

Just as I think I will lose consciousness, I look up and standing before me is my sweet student Connie Jo, my very own Cindy Loo Who. Oblivious to all the chaos around her, Cindy Loo announces once again that Santa is coming soon. She looks precious and smiles more sweetly than before as a light falls from the library ceiling, giving her a heavenly glow.

Despite all the commotion, I can't take my eyes off Cindy Loo. Her innocence calms me. The grin on her face and the light in her eyes that Santa is coming soon and what that means to her deeply touches my heart.

I block out the chorus of "ugly alert" being sung by twenty-four kindergartners as they dance around the stacks. Looking beyond them, I focus on the large windows in the front of the room. Outside, large snowflakes are floating down silently and peacefully.

For a brief moment, Cindy Loo's sweet declaration that Santa is coming fills me with peace on earth and good will toward men. I feel her little hands on my face as she looks into my eyes and whispers once again. "Santa is coming soon."

Hugging her tight I say, "Yes, Santa is coming soon." Then I look at Cindy Loo and smile. Glancing toward the front of the library at the little pagans dancing in slow motion, singing their muffled Ugly Alert carol, I think to myself, "Yes, Santa is coming soon. For me, Santa cannot come soon enough."

Heart Smart

It's 9:00 a.m. and we haven't even started the Heart Smart Parties at school. I already feel like Comte de Reynaud from the movie *Chocolat*. In my favorite scene, the Comte de Reynaud is passed out in the window of the *Chocolat* Shoppe after having eaten the entire display of chocolate. He is found the next morning in the Chocolat Shoppe window surrounded by broken molds of candy and melted chocolate covering his face and hands. On Valentine's Day, my students give me cute valentine cards and because they know my affinity for chocolate, they generously add chocolate to my gift. When you watch *Chocolat* and get to the scene where Alfred Molina's character has his chocolate meltdown, picture me, a redheaded librarian, sprawled out across the circulation desk at the end of the day on February 14th.

Hope

Sometimes SIRI doesn't hear well. How do I know? As I text a parent about a situation with her child, I say one simple word: HOPE. Then I press SEND.

SIRI hears: HO.

For the record: I did not call this mother a HO. I know I speak clearly, so SIRI must have a sense of humor. Just in case this parent doesn't have a sense of humor, I follow up with a phone call.

I Believe in Magic

Kindergarten can be an adjustment for students, especially for those who don't attend preschool. It's the first time they're away from home. They're thrown in to a mix of children they don't know, and we give them instructions they aren't always sure how to follow. Most handle it well. Some do not.

"I want my mommy," Toni says as she begins to cry. We are settling down in the library to reading time. Surely an engaging story will help calm her fears.

"It's okay, honey. You can sit by me. I am a mommy," I say with comfort in my voice.

Toni stops crying, takes a step back, and puts her hand up making sure to keep distance between us. She opens her eyes wide, tilts her head to the side, and stares me down as she sways back and forth.

"I believe in magic," she says slowly. "I believe that I'm still sleeping." Holding her breath, she looks at me for a moment, pauses, and starts to cry again.

"Okay then," I say, thinking about how this five-year-old is creeping me out. "Let's have story time!" Then she joins her class on the floor as if nothing has happened.

The Librarian Who Evolved

I look out across the library shelves and remember my first year as a librarian when I am very concerned about the order of the books. If they weren't shelved perfectly, I would develop a twitch. I could look out from my desk and with an eagle eye say, "See that book on the top row, third book over? It's out of place. Move it to the second shelf, fourth book in." I learned to do that from my mentor, Nancy Wilson. She is a master at organization. Then I would tell my students that I like "beautiful shelves, not ugly." For the proper effect, I would say "ugly" in my best Southern accent.

As time has gone by, though, I have learned that an ugly shelf is a well-explored shelf—and that brings me joy! Now I still tell students I like beautiful, not ugly shelves. And at the end of each school year, Mr. Dewey would be proud of the perfectly ordered stacks of books in my library. Throughout the year, however, the stacks will be ugly, which means I'm doing my job.

The Word on the Street

The word on the street is that Mrs. Eberst knows everything about Pokémon. "She has the best cards ever," they all say. Yes, I have the best Pokémon cards, thanks to eBay and a seller from Hong Kong. When it comes to trading, I must use my finest acting skills and pretend I know what I'm doing.

Taking a moment to ponder, I ask the first kid, "Is that the best you can do?" He usually breaks and offers me something else. Now I'm on the lookout for the Mega Mewtwo EX and the Tyranitar Spirit. Having both will surely make me every student's favorite teacher in the building.

Wilderness Survival Tips

I grew up in the grand state of Wyoming. My friends and I spent all our time outdoors riding horses, hiking in the mountains, and playing in the creek. We would camp year-round, sleeping in tents or in the open air, even digging snow caves in the middle of the winter. As a kid, I loved it. As I've grown older, I have become accustomed to city life and find that roughing has become a Holiday Inn with a pool and a pizza.

Each year my school takes our fourth graders to camp. Many of our students have never slept in a cabin in the woods where it's very dark at night, and you don't hear sounds of automobiles driving down your street.

One year, I am given the choice to teach either Pioneer Life or Outdoor Survival to our fourth-grade campers. "I'm so sorry," I said, graciously declining the class on outdoor survival. "My cell phone doesn't get reception in the woods." (And besides, how could I possibly teach children to call the Holiday Inn for a room or order a pizza?)

I'm Here for Donations

I loan a bucket to a third-grade teacher for a science experiment. Instead of holding it for her, I deliver it directly to her classroom. Walking into the room, I hold up the bucket and announce that I am here for donations. Two students get out of their seats and collect their book bags from their cubby. They come back with money, and without question, they deposit dollar bills in the bucket. By the time I reach the teacher's desk with the bucket, I have $4.00 in cash.

I had no idea supplementing my retirement would be so simple.

A Woman My Age

A woman my age should not jump rope at recess duty without Depends™.

You Are Giving Me Gray Hair!

Testing week, and the children are restless! My students feel the pressure in the air: a combination of relief that they've completed their morning tests mingled with the barometric pressure of incoming weather brings on uncontrollable-kid energy.

"You guys are killing me! You're going to make my hair turn gray!"

"You don't have gray hair, Mrs. Eberst. You have red hair!" says Leeann, rolling her eyes at me.

"Not for long! Look at what your class is doing to me." I pull my hair back to expose my gray roots, proving I need to make monthly visits to the beauty parlor. "Look!" I say overdramatically. "This happened just this period!"

Leeann's eyes grow wide. Then she covers her mouth with her hand. Not only is she quiet the remainder of class, she walks around the library telling other students they need to sit down and read.

"Trust me," she says. "It's important!"

You Think You've had A Bad Day?

It drives me crazy when I can't get a song lyric out of my head. The song is usually the theme to an old TV show I saw as a kid. For some reason, this day the *Beverly Hillbillies* invades my brain: "Come and listen to a story about a man named Jed. A poor mountaineer barely kept his family fed. Then one day he is shooting at some food, when up through the ground came a bubbling crude." At any given moment, I find myself distracted, tapping my toe and humming that theme song. Suddenly, in the middle of a staff meeting, the lyrics drop down from my head right out of my mouth, and in front of a disgruntled principal, I shout, "Oil that is, black gold, Texas tea . . . ." The principal is stunned, but she's used to my zaniness, and I still have my job.

When words stick with me like this, they're not always a song. Sometimes a line from a book or a movie will fill my brain, chasing out all my other thoughts. On any day, for example, I could be shelving animal books, when the title of a specific book reminds me of a line in a movie. Not only can I think of nothing else, the words I'm thinking repeat over and over with an Australian accent that would make Meryl Streep envious. In this case, I laugh out loud as I continue shelving books while quoting Crocodile Dundee: "So I oughta, mate! Sneaking up on a man when he's rendering first aid to a lady."

On this Australian accent day of mine, a student named Gail rushes into the library telling me, "I know I have an overdue book, but my teacher says I have to have a book in class today, or I'll be in trouble. Please let me get a book," she says, begging for a break. "I promise to bring back my overdue book tomorrow."

"You have an overdue book or books?" I ask. I could tell by the sound of her voice and the look on her face that she's desperate.

"Please, Mrs. Eberst. It's been a really bad day."

I understand bad days and what desperation feels like, so in my best Australian accent, I hold the book I'm about to shelve, look Gail right in the eye and say, "You think you've had a bad day? A dingo et maw baby!" Poor Gail doesn't know what to say. She has no idea what I'm talking about and looks at me both confused and concerned. It's hard for me to keep a straight face.

"Go, check out a book," I chuckle, not knowing if it's her expression that makes me laugh or the Australian accent rolling around in my head. I go back to shelving books and with every book I place on the shelf, I joyfully repeat, "A dingo et maw baby!"

Mantra for Teachers

Their brains are not fully developed yet.

Their brains are not fully developed yet.

Their brains are not fully developed yet.

Their brains are not fully developed yet.

STEM Day

- 1 bald cap
- 2 rubber ears
- 1 pair of goggles
- 1 pair of plaid tights
- 1 pair of rubber gloves
- A scooter

No, Mrs. Eberst is not planning a date night with her husband. Tomorrow she will be transformed into Dr. Nafario for STEM day.

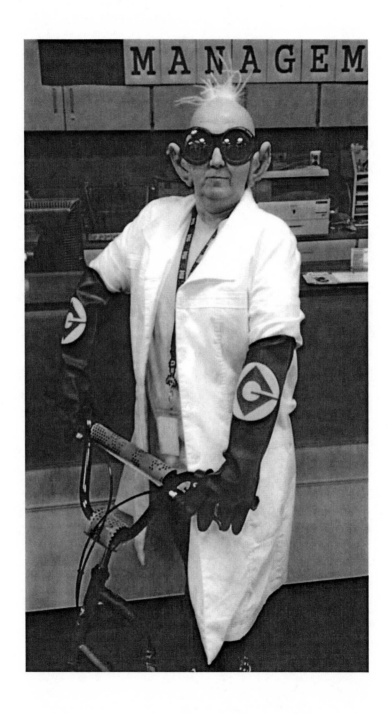

2

Adventures in
Learning and Fun

As a librarian, the Summit STEM Living Library Museum is my classroom. Thanks to the support of a Battelle STEM Grant, this once little library has been transformed into a Library Museum of vintage technology and fun. Students not only curate the collections, they curate their own learning. This student-designed-and-led library museum is for innovative learners. In fact, innovation is our theme and focus. It's a place where students experience adventure and have fun. Kindergartners can walk into a phone booth, and with just a little curious exploration, ask, "How do you text?" In our living library, 45 rpm records introduce children to Elvis, the Beatles, and Frank Sinatra. They can also sit at a black-and-white TV and challenge each other to a game of Pong on an old Atari.

The Living Library Museum is not typical. It's certainly not the library I grew up visiting as a child. When new students arrive and I ask them what they know about a library, they always tell me, "You have to be quiet." Children are delighted (as their parents look on a bit concerned) when I explain that Summit is not a quiet library. Most days, it's quite loud. Located in the middle of the building at the heart of the school and without doors, the sounds of learning from my library classroom reverberate down the halls. On occasion, so much learning is going on that my phone will ring, and the teacher on the other end will politely ask if we can hold it down. Whenever I remember that testing is going on in the building, I feel obliged to do so, but on normal days, I apologize and ask my students to tone it down a bit, all while knowing full well that the teacher will probably call again. When he does, I repeat the apology and joyfully remind him my transformed philosophy about elementary school libraries is that they're active places of play and discovery. In other words, "Learning should be heard!"

Libraries are no longer just a place to go for quiet reading. Learning should be a fun adventure, whether in a classroom or a library. Whether students are sitting on the floor playing with old telephones, hearing scary stories in a dark room, or competing in an Elvis Presley Impressionist Contest, learning takes place when students are engaged in fun. Maker Spaces in all forms provide engaging and challenging opportunities for learning. The Exploration Stations at Summit Living Library Museum provide kids experiences with not only vintage technology but vintage toys and board games. I find adults have just as much fun reliving their youth through exploring as their children do, and I hope you have as much fun reading these adventurous stories as we had living them.

Fiction Excuses Only

Notice: If you forget your library book, I am no longer giving you the evil eye or the Librarian Lecture as long as you can tell me the best possible story about why you forgot it. "I left it at home" or "I just forgot" doesn't cut it with me anymore. Although these are acceptable nonfiction excuses, they're too common. They don't show me any creative storytelling skills. Quite honestly, as a reader and a librarian, your worn-out excuses bore me.

It's time to practice "creative fictional thinking," which, I hope, will pay off for you during the writing portion of your state test. If you can not tell me something that demonstrates your imagination, then I will not make the effort to give you the evil eye or waste my energy giving you a Librarian Lecture that will just go in one of your ears and out the other.

Try something like the explanation Caleb gave for his missing book:

> *Vladimir Putin kidnapped me from Eastern Europe while I was researching WWII. He held me in Russia and made me eat sauerkraut until my mother rescued me. Because the two of us could barely escape, we didn't have time to get my book, but Putin promised he would send it soon by mail with a Russian postage stamp!*

Now THAT story is worthy of applause from your classmates and an enthusiastic, "Well done! Just bring your book tomorrow!"

from your school librarian. My only problem now is that students keep purposely forgetting their books just to share a story.

Musical Library Line

I am forever amazed at the importance children put on being first in line. The time that it takes for 25 students to get to the library, the cafeteria, or the lunchroom is the same regardless of the position in the line students find themselves. I spend much of my time dealing with serious concerns such as the following: "I am in line first," "It's not fair," or "He cut in front of the line." Managing whining and tattling is not in my lesson plan. Instead, I'm supposed to teach students to see a problem and then solve it.

One student in a particular class constantly repeats "I am first in line" every time his class visits the library. Brian believes in standing up for his rights. If something doesn't go his way, he thinks his rights are being violated. I need to fix this problem once and for all because he needs to know that when it comes to the library, I'm at the top of the food chain, no debating allowed. This line of thinking follows my other library rules: No whining. No tattling. If there's a problem, fix it.

"I am in line first," says Brian, as he pushes other students out of the way. "He cut. She cut. This isn't fair."

"Brian, you sound like a broken record," I tell him for the umpteenth time. "This is exactly what you said last week and the week before. No matter where you are in line, you still get to check out the library books that are in your hands. You're a STEM student. You've been a STEM student for three years. Now this should be no surprise to you, but our core values including patience and kindness have not changed. Follow them!"

Brian looks as though he's sure I want to debate our school expectations with him, and he's determined to prove that when the expectations were set, all the other student's needs were considered but not his. For a moment, I get lost in a dream of installing a small red box with numbered tickets just like the one at the local butcher shop. I imagine telling him to pick a number. Instead, I take a step back, look at everyone in line, and announce, "Today we will use the design cycle and redesign the library line!"

Then I tell the students at the circulation desk not to check one more book out to another student until we have solved this real world problem.

"Chloe," I say to the girl in the front of the line, "I'm going to move you here. This is a better spot for you." I move Chloe down two spaces. I put Brian second in line, which pleases him. Then I step back, fold my arms, and pretend I'm thinking. Then I quickly begin switching students around. "Carol, you trade places with Gordon. Harvey, you switch with Carol." This move puts Brian at the front of the line. The other students in line roll their eyes, groan, and whisper something about this not being fair. I look at the line again and remind everyone to be patient as we are still in the design process.

The self-satisfied smirk on Brian's face disappears when I announce that Chloe is better suited for the front of the line behind Carol and in front of Gordon and Harvey. This moves Brian back four spots. I go on like this for about five minutes. Most students are good-natured about the musical library line, especially when I pull them from their place in line, put them in a new spot, and announce joyfully that this spot is custom made for them.

"You look marvelous here, Jim!"

"Carla, I thought you belonged there, but now I see that you were meant to stand here."

Finally, I stand back, look over the line and proclaim, "Job done! We have designed the perfect library line!" My students nod in agreement and patiently wait as I give the all clear for the student librarians to begin checking out books. Realizing it's best not to open his mouth, Brian glares at me from his place at the back of the line. He knows this is one argument he cannot win.

Zombies

First graders are always forgetting our school's expectations. The long wide hallways are so inviting, you would think we installed a light from a racetrack that counts down to green and drops a checkered flag, giving them all permission to run. I'm constantly reminding students to walk. Standing at the entrance to the library watching Finn and Owen run full speed down the hall, I ask, "What are you doing?"

"We're going to the play!" Owen says, slowing down to a brisk walk when he sees me. He makes me think of how I drive with my lead foot, quickly slowing down the minute I see a police car.

"Do you know what we expect when you're in the halls?"

"Walking," says Finn, out of breath. I remind them what can happen when they run in the halls. "We don't want you to get hurt," I say, "whether you're walking with your class or by yourself." Suddenly, I feel pangs of guilt as I listen to my well-rehearsed lecture, thinking I need to apply it to my own driving, so I say, "You need to walk unless we tell you to run out of the building."

"Like a fire?" asks Owen.

"Yes," I say. "Like a fire."

"And zombies," Finn adds.

"Yes, Finn, you may run if there are zombies."

After this conversation with kids, I promise myself to slow down when I drive, unless there are zombies. Then I can speed up.

Thank You, Diana Ross

A chatty group of students are cause for me to stand up and burst into song, complete with choreography:

STOP! Talking in my class, before you break my heart.
STOP! Talking in my class, before you break my heart.
Think it Oh oh ver.
Think it Oh oh ver.
STOP!

The fourth graders look at me like I have totally lost my mind. But it works. They stop talking. Thank you Diana Ross and the Supremes for my new classroom management technique!

The Best Homework Ever

After reading *Iggy Peck, Architect* by Andrea Beaty about a boy who builds anything out of everything, I give my students the following homework: Your homework must be completed at dinner. Your assignment is to look at the plate of food before you engineer a design. You can stack the chicken nuggets to make a building, or you can dig a hole in your mashed potatoes to make a volcano. Peas make good lava. You can create any design you want.

Challenge Expectations:

You have to tell your parents what you are doing.
You can't use your fingers unless it is finger food.
You can't play just to play.
You must be creative.
You have to eat it. Clean your plate.

With her eyes lit up, Heidi says, "This is the best homework ever!" Nick, on the other hand, claims, "My parents will yell at me." Louise, a future Chopped Champion asks, "Can I get extra things from the fridge?"

I repeat the challenge expectations as other questions from my students come flying toward me: "I'm not doing this. I'm grounded already." "You can't make me do this. My parents will be mad at you."

Rolling her eyes, Christine insists, "You guys aren't any fun!"

I ask the kids to take a picture of their design and have their parents e-mail it to me tonight. "Let's see how many Iggy Pecks we have in this class!" I say. The next morning my email is filled with photos from last night's dinner showing me how creative or how inhibited each student can be.

Thank You. Thank You Very Much

In the library museum, we house a collection of vintage technology. One of our items is a record player with a collection of albums. The students love exploring the records from Ricky Nelson to the Blues Brothers. On this day, I am introducing first graders to Elvis. The class begins with listening and dancing to "Jailhouse Rock" and ends with a contest selecting the student who can do the best Elvis impression.

"How many of you have heard of Elvis Presley?" I ask. I'm met with blank stares.

"Do you mean Elvis?" asks a confused Kathleen. After her question, several students raise their hands showing that they have indeed heard of Elvis.

"There is no Presley in his name," says Kathleen. "His name is Elvis."

"She's right," says Wendi. "My grandma loves Elvis. That's his name." Kathleen is happy that her friend Wendi gave the right answer, so she tells her thank you. I curl my bottom lip and stand up, wiggle my hips, and in my best Elvis impression, say, "Don't you mean 'Thank you, Thank you very much!'" These first graders look at me having no idea what I'm doing or why I'm thanking them, including the Elvis fans.

Kathleen speaks for her classmates, saying, "You are kinda weird today." The rest of the class agrees. I curl my lips again, and as I put on "Jailhouse Rock" I say, once again, "Thank you. Thank you very much."

My Finest Performance

My finest acting gig happens while a fourth grade class visits the library. I have a handful of students who are not putting in their time or passing lessons in our school's blended-learning program. These students have been with us since kindergarten, so they know the drill.

In an Oscar-worthy performance, I fall to my knees. With my head down, I sob, telling the boys that my heart is broken. "I sob tears for you my darlings!" Then I moan so convincingly that a student puts her hand on my shoulder, assuring me that she is reading and passing the lessons. "It's okay, Mrs. Eberst," she says, "I passed."

I look up at her, jump to my feet, and perform a cheerleading routine. Beginning with my arms stretched upward, I begin kicking my feet, chanting, "I passed lessons 1, 2, 3. No more tears! Only cheer! Give me an R!" The girls in the class yell, "R" and continue with each letter until we all cheer the word "READ!"

Only real pom-poms would have enhanced our performance. I also would have attempted the splits, but I knew I never would have gotten back up. Most of the girls jump up and down cheering, but my two less-than-committed boys look at each other in agreement: "Bonkers," they say. "Total bonkers."

Bonkers or not, let's see how many more blended-learning lessons get completed next week.

Nocturnal?

Rocky loves books about birds, owls in particular. He doesn't check out books on any other topic. He works very hard to understand everything he can, including the proper vocabulary. When it comes to birds, he's advanced for a second grader.

Holding an open book in his hands, Rocky asks me, "What is a day-urinal?"

"Say it again?" I ask.

"You know, a day-urinal. Is it an antonym of nocturnal?

I must have a puzzled look on my face because he goes on to explain that animals who hunt at night are nocturnal, so it only makes sense to him that animals who hunt during the day must be day-urinal.

"That is a very good question. You should research the answer here in the library. I will be very interested to see what you find," still thinking to myself how much sense that makes to me, too!

Scary Stories You Tell in the Dark

Every October I take my fourth-grade classes to my workroom in the back of the library. There's only one way in and one way out, with no window to let in even a drop of light. Once inside, I turn off the lights and hold the flashlight up to my chin, letting the glow eerily reflect off my face. There, in the darkness of the back room, I read Alvin Schwartz's *Scary Stories You Tell in the Dark.*

What have I learned from this October adventure? Fourth-grade boys scream like girls.

The Groan Heard Around the World

The groan heard around the world echoes through the halls as the principal announces, "There will be no more Pokémon cards in the building." Then a moment of hope stirs when she also announces, "Mrs. Eberst will continue to give Pokémon cards as incentives."

Phew! This saves me from having to go underground and trade in the black market (the back room of the library with an observant first grader standing watch). The principal continues, "Mrs. Eberst will find ways for students to earn the cards. If you get a Pokémon card from the library, it goes straight into your book bag and must go home."

Summit students are always encouraged to work hard, be kind, do their work, and follow the SPARK expectations. They never know when Mrs. Eberst will slip them a Mega Charzard EX or other exciting cards for which she spent her retirement.

As Glen walks into the library immediately after morning announcements, he asks another student, "Do you want to trade a Purrion for your Mew Two EX?"

"Didn't you hear Mrs. Drury's announcement?" I ask.

"I didn't think she was talking about me."

"She is," I tell him, pointing out his mistake.

"Okay," he says, "but if you're giving them away, I need a New Two EX." I tell him I will be watching his success in the building. If he's giving any away, I'm looking for a Mega Charzard EX 147 B Turbo Power. Glen gives me a blank stare as I add, "With heated seats."

"You don't know your Pokémon, do you?" Glen says.

"Perhaps I know more about them than you do!" I tell him. "I'll be watching you!"

How Deep Are the Wetlands?

We have wetlands behind our building as a part of our campus. We use them as an outdoor classroom and research area. Owen, a fourth grader, who thinks he knows more than his teachers, asks me if I know how deep the water is in the wetlands. He is pleased when I tell him that I have no idea, which justifies his belief that he knows more than I do.

"Really?" he says sarcastically," I thought librarians knew everything." I tell him that we don't know everything, but we know how to find the answers to everything!

Owen thinks this will be a good challenge and says, "I bet you don't know how to find out how deep the wetlands are, do you?"

I think this is a grand opportunity to match Owen's sarcasm, so I politely suggest that he walk out to the middle of the wetlands to see if the water level is over his head.

Do Your Job!

The early morning crowd has gathered waiting for the bell to ring. Students run off the bus and push their way to the door, so they can be the first in for breakfast. As I say good morning to students, I see Roger plowing his way through the crowd, pushing others out of his way like a bowling ball knocking down pins. He is a young man on a mission.

Making his way to me, he says, "There are two students back there pushing each other. Go do your job!"

"Yes, sir!" I say, saluting and thanking him for demonstrating exactly the same pushing behavior on his way to report the poor behavior of other students!

The Hardest Part of The Job

My student librarians take their job very seriously. With my expert training, they master checking books in and out for their library patrons. Some demonstrate better customer service than others. Elizabeth, for example, is checking books out to her class, but when the phone at my desk rings, she doesn't know what to do. They don't have phones like this at her house, only cell phones. She looks panicked, searching the library for me, trying to figure out this old technology.

"The phone won't stop ringing," she shouts. I am busy working with students and shout back for her to answer it. She picks up the receiver and freezes.

"Where is the talk button?" she asks, holding the receiver to her ear.

"There is no talk button," I instruct her. "Just say hello." Not sure what to do, Elizabeth begins talking so quickly, I think she will hyperventilate.

"Hello. Reynoldsburg Schools Summit Road Living Library Museum. This is Elizabeth," she rambles without taking a breath. "What do you want?" Silently staring at the receiver, she holds the phone in her hand. "I think they hung up," she says.

"If it's important, they'll call back," I assure her.

Looking pale, Elizabeth tells me, "I don't know how you do this job. Answering the phone is the hardest part of being a librarian!

Prank Calls

A part of the Summit Library is our "Makers Space" called the "Exploration Station." One of the stations has a variety of old telephones for students to explore. Some are push button, some are rotary, and the most popular is the Snoopy phone. This station is filled with opportunities to stretch one's imagination.

A group of boys sit in a circle each holding a telephone and laugh hysterically. I sit down on the floor next to them and ask what they are doing.

"Making prank phone calls," Jeff answers with a smile.

I listen as the boys pretend to make calls. Jeff presses the numbers on the rotary phone. I tell him he'd have better results if he *dialed* the number. The phone is not push button. Fascinated by his new skill using a vintage telephone, he dials a number.

"Hello. Can I talk to your mom?" he giggles and then hangs up. The boys laugh. Jeff is pleased with himself. Mike tells them that he knows how to make a real prank call because he saw it on an old TV show once. He picks up the push button phone telling his friends that this is much faster. After pressing numbers, he speaks into the receiver. "Hello. Is your refrigerator running? Hurry up and catch it before it gets away!" He hangs up the phone and the boys throw themselves back on the floor in a fit of laughter.

"Is that the best you've got?" I ask them, telling them that when I was their age, I was a master at making prank calls. The key is to sound serious when they make the call, so the person answering the call won't suspect you are playing. I demonstrate.

Taking the rotary phone in hand, I begin to dial Fred's Market in Jackson Hole, Wyoming. I begin with 733 and continue to dial the number I still remembered after nearly 50 years. As a kid myself, I called that number often.

"Hello," I say sounding serious. "Do you have pickled pigs feet?"

The clerk responds with a polite, "Yes, we do."

Being unable to maintain my seriousness, just as I did back in 1967, I giggle and snort and can barely get the words out. "I'm sorry, but if you wear socks, no one will notice!"

The boys gain a new respect for me that day. I'm glad there was no such thing as caller ID when I was a kid, taking the opportunity to explain to them that in the 21st Century, making anonymous prank calls is no longer possible. However, by the look on their faces, I suspect that every grocery store in central Ohio will be getting a call that evening.

3

Adventures in Reading

A former student, Ayah, comes to me when she is about to graduate from high school to tell me that before meeting me in the third grade, she always hated to read. "When you told me about the Magic Tree House series by Mary Pope Osborne, I started reading and never looked back." Revelations like that always make me happy that I have inspired children to love reading.

I admit, though, that I'm always concerned when a student tells me they don't picture anything when they read. They often report that their minds are blank, which is apparent when I'm watching a class during silent reading and see their eyes wander around the room as they turn the pages of a book. When I see this happening, I might ask a student to read to me. Inevitably, he knows the words and is fluent, starting and stopping as the punctuation dictates, yet he lacks expression in his voice and his face while he reads. When I ask him what he reads, he might shrug his shoulders and look at me with the same blank expression. I tell him I can read the words in the medical journal but have no idea what I'm reading and will show the same made-up enthusiasm that he just showed me. To remedy this problem, I often say, "Follow me to the stacks. We are going exploring for an adventure."

In contrast, it's exciting to me when I see students really reading. They become oblivious to the distractions of their surroundings. In their faces and in their body language, they aren't just reading words; they are seeing, feeling, and living them. I know if students have just *read* the words in the book or if they have *lived* the story they read. When they return the book and I ask them, "Did you like it?" they will respond with their usual monotone, "Yah" or, to my delight, with an animated, "Yes!"

Without using their imaginations, children are only reading words and missing out on amazing adventures. I tell my students when I read, I make a movie in my head. I create the colors, smell the smells, orchestrate the sounds, design the costumes, and build the sets. Many times, I cast myself as the main character in the story and even go as far as to create an unwritten character, a friend to the protagonist. Like one day, I'm sharing the tools I use to make reading exciting when Patrick's hand shoots up. "I do that all of the time!" he says enthusiastically. By his expression, I know that he is living what he reads.

Another time, a first grader comes to my desk with a copy of Harry Potter. He is new to our building so I'm not sure of his ability. I find most first graders select their books not only using the "five finger rule" but by the size of the book. A very popular question first graders ask is, "Where do I find the big books?" When this new first grader comes to my desk with a big book, I ask him to read a page to me. He reads with expression, throwing in a few dramatic pauses. He doesn't rush. The words flow from one sentence to the next. He reads as though he and Harry Potter are the only two people in the room. I let him read for several pages because together, we are transported to Number 4 Privet Drive.

I have never read the words of a book to my students. To me, picture books are simply scripts to perform. I try to model living a book and hope young readers get swept away by inspiring authors and illustrators. When great writers partner with imaginative readers, there is no telling what will happen.

What Did You Do
in The Library Today?

One of my favorite read-a-louds is *Pete the Cat: I Lost My Groovy Buttons* by James Dean and Eric Litwin. You can hear us singing throughout the entire school, "I lost my groovy buttons," as we dance around the library. I've often wondered if the office is joining in through the security cameras.

Most days, fourth graders think they are too old for such frivolity, but today, the library is filled with uninhibited nine- and ten-year-olds. Throwing my arms back and singing "My buttons, my buttons. I lost my groovy buttons," I look down and notice that in my enthusiasm, the buttons of my shirt have come undone. There I am dancing in my glory, and I've lost my groovy buttons.

"Oops! Showing my boobs," I say without thinking, pulling my unbuttoned shirt closed. I start to laugh. Fourth graders gasp and laugh along with me. While I'm buttoning up my shirt, I laugh so hard that I begin to cry. Fourth graders are laughing so hard they are crying, too! The girls are shocked and I'm sure they're thinking, "Poor Mrs. Eberst." The boy's faces are red, and I don't want to know *what* they are thinking. We are all laughing so hard tears are streaming down our faces. All I can think about are the security cameras and how I'm going to get fired for this.

After gaining control of myself and of the class, sweet Anna tells me not to worry. "We didn't see anything." Debbie says she has never seen a teacher cry, and Todd announces that he has never heard a teacher use the word "boobs" before. I shudder anticipating what parents might say when their child answers the question, "What did you do in the library today, honey?"

Bad Kitty

The series *Bad Kitty* by Nick Bruel is a favorite among my first graders. It is one of the most requested titles and this day is no exception.

"Mithus Ezbert," asks Mikey. "Do you have bad tittys?"

They aren't bad for a woman my age, I so badly wanted to say, but instead, I walk him to the fiction section and help him find a copy of the book.

I'm Turning into Chocolate

Before students go to the stacks to find their library books, I read *Chocolatina* by Erik P. Kraft. When I finish reading, twenty-four excited first graders run from the reading corner to find their books. One lone student remains. She sits motionless and begins to cry. Concerned, I kneel down next to her and ask, "What's wrong?"

Pam looks up at me with tears streaming down her face. "I'm afraid I'm going to turn into chocolate," she cries. At first, I think she is kidding. I know I don't just read to my students but try to perform the books as I share them. Obviously, Pam is affected in a way I never imagined. I've had kids cry as I read *The Giving Tree*. I cry myself when I read *The Giving Tree* but never when I read *Chocolatina* about a girl who turns into chocolate.

"Oh, sweetheart, you will not turn into chocolate," I say with a chuckle. "*Chocolatina* is fiction. It isn't real. It is a story made up from the author's imagination." It takes her a moment to compose herself.

"Okay," she says, wiping her tears as she gets up to find her library books.

I go to my desk to help library workers when Kathryn walks over and tells me that Pam is still crying. She is standing in front of the picture book section, and I can see her shoulders moving up and down as she tries to catch her breath between sobs. I call her to my desk, put my hands on hers, and instead of calling her sweetie, take a friendly but firm approach. "What's wrong now?" I ask.

Unable to catch her breath, she tries to explain. "I, uh, can feel, uh, I am turning into uhh chocolate."

I am trying to be patient. Of all the days for this to happen, she picks a day where I am training first-grade librarians to run the circulation desk. I look at her and think to myself, "You have get to be kidding me. Really? Really! Didn't we just have this conversation?" Instead of saying what I am thinking, I take a deep breath and speak in what I hope will be a pleasant tone. "Pam, I think we just talked about this."

"But I'm really afraid I am turning into chocolate. Chocolatina loved chocolate, and she turned into a chocolate girl. I love chocolate, too, and now I'm turning into chocolate."

"Stop thinking about it," I say. "You are not turning into chocolate. I want you to go over to the table where Kathryn is sitting and read with her." Kathryn is my go-to girl, the student who is kind, studious, and helpful. She will help Pam focus on something else.

It didn't take long before Kathryn is at my desk. "Excuse me, Mrs. Eberst. May I move to another table?" she asks apologetically. "I can't read because Pam won't stop crying." I look over at Pam, still crying, wave her back to my desk, and hand her a box of Kleenex.

Patient no longer, I speak firmly. "Now look, sister, the book is fiction. That means it isn't real. If it were, then I would be worried. But it isn't, and I'm not. Besides, if anyone were going to turn into chocolate, it would be ME! I eat chocolate all the time. Do I look worried that I might turn into chocolate?" She shakes her head no. "That's right. I'm not worried because the book is fiction. Do I need to take a bite out of your arm to check? I know my chocolate, and I would know if you were turning into chocolate."

I grab Pam's arm, make munching sounds, and pretend to chew. She laughs. "Sorry, sister," I tell her. "You don't taste like chocolate to me." Pam takes a Kleenex, wipes her eyes, blows her nose, and skips off to the stacks without shedding another tear.

I Learned It from My Library Book

I am always thrilled when my students read a book and apply the knowledge they gain from their reading. An Origami book is recently returned with every other page folded into what is shown on that page. The attempt is impressive considering no pages are torn.

Another book is returned nearly torn in half. The book with the broken spine falls open to the section that reads, "How to Tear a Book in Half."

How can you argue with gaining knowledge by reading?

I Speak Alien

I watch Gary sitting on the floor with a book on his lap. He is holding up the middle finger on each hand. He looks at his open book and then makes the gestures to other students.

"What are you doing?" I ask.

"Nothing," He says. That is always the answer kindergartners give when I ask what they are doing, and they know they aren't doing what they are supposed to be doing. I sit on the floor next to Gary and ask what he is doing with his hands.

"Nothing," he says, again looking up at the ceiling. His round face turns a light shade of red.

"Sometimes there is a gesture we make with our hands that isn't very nice," I say. He wants to know what a 'guessed ur' is. I explain that sometimes we make a sign with our fingers. "This means peace" I tell him as I make the peace sign. He practices with his chubby little fingers and smiles. I go on to tell him that a gesture is a way to talk with our hands that sometimes our hands talk nice and sometimes they don't."

"Like this?" He makes a peace sign.

"Yes. That is nice."

"How about this?" He flips me off. I tell him that was something he shouldn't do because it isn't very nice. He seems satisfied with my explanation, picks up his book, and follows his friends in a straight kindergarten line back to class.

After his class leaves the library, I get a call from his teacher wanting to know what happened in class that day. I explain the sign language conversation I had with Gary. She tells me on the way back to class, not only did he flip off the entire fourth grade but get some of his classmates to join in. Picture four kindergarten boys, following hallway expectations by walking silently in a straight orderly line, then flipping the bird to everyone they pass. Parents are called, and kindergarten tears are shed. Gary is sternly reminded that Mrs. Eberst already explained to him that what he is doing isn't a good idea.

The next day a phone call comes in from mom. She explains that her son really didn't understand what the gesture means. She requests that I look on page 40 of his library book on Aliens. On page 40, there's a picture of an alien with a big head and bulgy eyes. His long arms support oversized hands, which he holds up to be the focal point of the picture. On each hand are three fingers. One long finger reaching up with shorter fingers on each side. Mom explains her son is not flipping off the fourth grade. Tearfully, he told her, "I am speaking alien to all the children that passed me in the hall. It's in my library book!"

Whatever Turns You On

I walk a fine line between insisting that my students check out books that they can read and finding things that will turn them on. I know each student's reading range and have always insisted that they check out at least one book that falls on their level. I'm always telling them, "You can't get turned on by reading if you don't understand what you read." However, in the same breath, I tell students they have to explore. "If you find something you're attracted to, then you should give it a try, regardless of the reading level."

As I watch my students explore, I'm taken back to the days of my youth when I would ride my bike to the Teton County Library every Saturday to pick up as many Nancy Drew books that would fit into the basket of my purple Schwinn. As much as I loved Nancy Drew, the day I get turned on to reading came when I found my way to the back of the log cabin library and took the three steps down to the nonfiction stacks. I remember sitting for hours exploring the shelves filled with subjects I had never heard of before. My rather sheltered life as an elementary student in the late 1960s is blown wide open by the books on those shelves. I want my students to find out through our libraries, either our own school library or the public library, that there's a whole new world out there to be discovered in books.

James is one of many students who decides to take me at my word. After spending most of his time in the library searching the shelves, he asks rather sheepishly, "This book is higher than my reading level. Can I check it out?"

"Do you want to try it?" I ask as I thumb the pages being sure to keep my eyes on his face. The look in a student's eyes speaks louder than the words they utter. "It is a bit higher than your range. How bad do you want to try it?"

"I want to try it. It turns me on." His eagerness to try the book matches the sparkle in his eyes.

"It turns you on? I ask. "Who taught you that?"

"You did."

"Yes, I did James! Go check it out."

"Thank you, Mrs. E.," he smiles, pleased with himself. "You are a marvelous woman."

"Thank you," I agree. "Who taught you that?"

"You did!" James shouts over his shoulder on his way to the circulation desk.

Smiling, I say to myself, "Yes, I did!"

There's No Crying in the Library

Every November I read my favorite Thanksgiving book, *Thanksgiving at the Tappletons* by Eileen Spinelli. This book touches my heart. The story always chokes me up and brings tears to my eyes. I had no idea reading it to a group of students would end in such a debacle. I come to the part in the story where the Tappletons, after losing their Thanksgiving dinner to a variety of mishaps, declare that the holiday isn't ruined because, "After all, we have each other." My voice cracks and tears fill my eyes. Before I know it, tears are flowing down my cheeks.

Looking confused, Payten asks, "Are you crying, Mrs. Eberst? You are really a good actress because you look like you are really crying." His confusion turns to concern when he asks the boy sitting next to him, "Is she really crying?" When he knows that the tears are not an act, he reaches out and pats my knee trying to comfort me.

"Wait a minute," Steve shouts, "When I got upset about forgetting my library book, you told me there was no crying in the library!"

"This isn't the same thing as forgetting your library book," I say as I try to explain how much this story means to me and why I am being so emotional. I can tell by their faces and behaviors they aren't sure how to handle these emotions.

"Fine," I say. "Repeat after me: Mrs. Eberst, don't be such a boob!" I know as soon as I say "boob" that my word choice will not work with second graders. This is a group of kids who love to talk about body parts and bodily functions. "Now listen," I tell them. "I didn't say *boobs*." I said, "Don't be a boob. Hasn't anyone ever heard someone say that when you're crying?"

The boys look at each other and smile while the girls giggle. Jerry, who never pays attention, looks at his shocked classmates and wants to know what he missed. Exasperated, I throw my hands in the air and say, "How old are you people?" In unison, the class shouts as if I should already know the answer, "Eight!"

"Well, that explains everything," I say. "Forget you learned a new vocabulary word and go find your library books." As students run to the stack, my friend Jerry stays back, smiles at me and says, "Have a nice Thanksgiving, Mrs. E."

I smile and a bit teary-eyed, say, "Thanks, Jerry. Happy Thanksgiving."

Spiders Are Evil and Eat People

I am assigned to work with Jonathon on his reading. He hates to focus. He always has something more interesting to talk about than the subject at hand. He can always find a reason why doing what needs to be done doesn't need to be done! As we read together, he wanders off expressing random thoughts. I am assigned to him because I can usually follow these thoughts.

"We need to get through one more book before you go back to class," I tell him. The truth is we need to get through an entire book. I reach over and grab a book about spiders. Boys like spiders, and this should keep his interest, right? One look at the book, he pushes his chair away from the table, and throws his arms up in the air.

"No! No! NO!" I can't read that book. I don't know how to read!" he shouts.

I explain to him that we just read something together and that he is brilliant.

"No! I can't read a book about spiders. I hate spiders! They are mean. They are evil and they eat people!"

"What if I put my hand over the picture of the spider?" I ask, placing my hand over the photograph of the tarantula. "Then all you will see are the words."

"That works," he says, bringing his chair back to the table, enthusiastically reading the book.

I, on the other hand, am feeling a bit tense. I tremble and nearly break out in a sweat thinking about my hand over the picture of the tarantula. I'm reliving the rage I felt when a large spider hung on a towel on the floor in my laundry room. I threw both the towel and the spider into the washing machine, turning it on extra hot and slamming the lid shut. I also have memories of a large wolf spider that ran across my living room floor the night before and how, without reason, I emptied an entire can of RAID on him to guarantee the wolf spider's demise. Then I remembered while in elementary school running and screaming at recess to get away from the hundreds of black spiders and their webs as they blew across our playground in the spring breeze.

While processing all these random memories about my own encounters with spiders, I try to listen as Jonathan reads, but all I can think about is that I, too, hate spiders. They are mean. They are evil, and they eat people!

The Blue Whale

When I read the book, *Billy Twitters and His Blue Whale Problem* by Mac Barnett, I notice my second graders have trouble visualizing how long a blue whale is. It takes twenty-four students averaging 4 feet in height lying head to toe on the library floor to demonstrate the length of a blue whale. We run out of room before we reach the 100 feet needed.

Lesson Learned

It takes Justin no time at all to find his library books. He knows exactly where the *Goosebumps* books by R.L. Stein are on the shelf. He is particular about which order he will read them and gets frustrated if the copy he wants is not on the shelf. I explain to him that the books aren't written in a specific order but stand alone as a story. "There are no sequels," I tell him. He doesn't understand what a sequel is since it's not part of his first-grade vocabulary. "I don't read books about squeak whales," he says, explaining he doesn't like stories about fish.

Running to the stacks to get his books, Justin shouts, "There aren't any *Goosebumps* books left! What the %(#!" The word he shouts rhymes with an animal on Old MacDonald's farm who sang, "Quack, quack here and a quack, quack there." The shouted word stops other first graders in their tracks. The entire class looks at me to see what I'm going to do.

"Excuse me, what did you say?"

"I said, there are no more *Goosebumps* books. What the…" I stop him just in time before he causes the boys to gasp for air and the girls to faint. "Don't repeat it," I say. "Did you say what I thought you said?" He puts his head down and whispers, "Yes." Then he tells me that the word was on the tip of his tongue and just fell out when he opened his mouth.

"What will your mother say when I call her?" I ask him, which makes him start to cry. "I have a feeling you know what she is going to say. Did you learn that word at home?" He tells me that he learned it at school, and his mother is not going to be very happy.

"I'm sure she won't be," I tell him. "Justin, there are better words to say than the one you chose. That is not a word anyone should use, especially nice boys like you. Let's practice what we could have said instead. You need to have different words on the tip of your tongue, so when you open your mouth, better words fall out."

I tell him to practice these new words instead: "Holy Toledo!"

Justin repeats, "Holy Toledo!"

"Doggone it!" I say.

"Doggone it!" he says.

Then I tell him to try my favorite: "Zap-a-doody."

"Zap-a-doody!" he says. "I like that one," laughing when he says it. I tell him to practice and hear him say, "There are no more *Goosebumps* books left! Zap-a-doody!"

Lesson learned.

May I Go to The Loo?

I am always telling my students that it is important to apply what they have learned from the library books that they check out or from the books that I read to them. Through read-a-louds, we learn, for example, that students can no longer ask to use the restroom; they must ask in their best British accent: "May I go to the loo, please?" This is thanks to the new vocabulary in Sean Taylor's *Robot Rumpus*. Similarly, thanks to *Sixteen Cows* by Lisa Wheeler, if a student is upset, she must respond in her best cowboy accent with "That really gets my goat!"

In other words, we speak "children's literature" in the library.

They Got Gypped

Some students don't quite get the message behind an author's story. They have their own ideas about the conclusion of the plot. Their alternative conclusions are always a delight, especially if the students are six years old. For example, a story I enjoy reading and talking about with my classes is *Rude Giants* by Audrey Wood. The story is about how two rude giants kidnap Gerta the Cow. Gerta's friend Beatrix the butter maid saves the cow by telling the rude giants that they can't eat the finest cow in all the land without making a few changes to their lifestyle. They live in a messy castle, gobble their food, speak unkindly, and quite frankly, need a personal makeover.

Beatrix explains to the giants that the cow will taste much better if they clean up their castle, learn manners, and take small bites of their food. She goes on to tell them that the cow will taste better if they make themselves beautiful. They do these things and suddenly think differently about eating Gerta, for how could such polite, beautiful giants who live in a clean castle possibly eat a cow as kind as Gerta? The story concludes with the townspeople gathering up their food and taking it to the castle to share with the giants who no longer scare them. Most children love the end of this story, except Chip.

"What?" he asks. "They didn't eat the cow? It would have been a better story if they ate the cow. They cleaned their castle, learned manners, and took a bath, and they *still* didn't get to eat the cow? They should have eaten the cow. They got gypped!"

I Have Weird Parents

I read *Weird Parents* by Audrey Wood to all my kindergartners. When finished, I tell them that my children have weird parents and share stories with them of waking Katie and Joe up with show tunes, shouting to the neighborhood through open windows that the Eberst children are getting out of bed. I also tell them about how we used to sit in the van, and I would cover my mouth with my hand so my voice was muffled when I'd ask, "Welcome to McDonald's. May I take your order?" My delighted children would place their order, and we would laugh. My favorite is going grocery shopping and picking up an item from the shelf, then making up a commercial for the product and asking my children if that's something we should buy.

I ask my group of five-year-olds if they have weird parents, too. Scott raises his hand. "My parents are weird. They are always playing with each other." I couldn't resist. I just had to ask, "What kind of games do they play?"

Rolling his eyes, David says, "They are always grabbing each other's butts." The girls act as if they are embarrassed, while the boys take advantage of David speaking first, giving them permission to repeat the word "butt" over and over. I give them the "that's enough" look, and they stop their chorus of the "b" word, feeling rather proud of themselves for being so daring in the school library. Tommy looks over at David and says, "They *are* weird parents."

The best part? This child's parents are divorced. There's nothing like getting along for the sake of the children.

The First Lady of the United States of America

I read *President Taft is Stuck in the Bath*, which is wonderfully written by Mac Barnett and illustrated by Chris Van Dusen. The first time reading the book, I didn't know it would cause such a commotion for a class of second graders. The chaos began the moment I explained that President Taft was a very large man. Donna raised her hand and asks if he is as large as I am. She is saved from my sarcastic response by Shane, a self-proclaimed scholar of President Taft getting stuck in his bathtub as he began his lecture on 1910 politics and the very large bathtub put in the White House.

All I want is to share this story, but I'm unprepared for the drama that follows. I will paraphrase the author's story: "Two hours passed. The water got cold and President Taft was stuck in the bath. Someone knocked at the door. 'Double blast,' said Taft. 'Blast and draft.' 'Oh dear, it was Taft's wife, the First Lady of the United States of America."

"Michelle Obama is the First Lady!" shouts Sherri.

"Yes, Sherri, you are correct. Michelle Obama is THE First Lady now in 2016. But in 1910, there was another First Lady."

That time difference means nothing to Sherri. Shaking her head, she insists, "No! No! No! Michelle Obama is the First Lady."

Shane, the Taft scholar, rolls his eyes at Sherri and jumps in. "It is 1910, and Michelle Obama isn't even born yet."

"There have been many men who have served as President of the United States," I add. Before I can finish, students begin to shout out the names of the presidents they know: George Washington, Abraham Lincoln, Barack Obama! "Yes," I say, "and each one of those presidents had a wife. The President's wife is the First Lady."

"That's what I said, Michelle Obama!" says Sherri, losing patience.

She isn't the only one losing patience. I speak slowly and directly. "Yes, but in *this* story, the President's wife, Mrs. Taft, is the First Lady."

With the tone and passion of a Southern minister and with a hand firmly on her hip and the other pointing straight at me, Sherri sings, "Michelle OOOOOO BAAAAA MAHHHH!" This, of course, inspires Donna, who is sitting next to Sherri. Donna puts her hand on her hip, tilts her head to the side, and shouts, "Uh Huh! That's right!" Then Sherri turns to her classmate sitting in the reading corner and proclaims, "Michele, Ohhhhh. Baaaaaa. Mah. Is. The. First. Lady. Of. The. United. States. Of. America." In unison both girls tilt their heads to the side and look at me with a "so there" look.

About this time, Shane is also losing his patience. "Can't we just get back to the story about the bathtub?" he says, rolling his eyes once again. I continue to read: "My love," says Taft, "I'm stuck in the bath."

"So, you are, said the First Lady."

Before I can go any farther, Sherri and Donna give another rousing chorus of "Michellleeee Obammma." Shane rolls his eyes again, throws his hands in the air, and surrenders to all sense of historical fact. The other students begin to giggle because in the illustration, President Taft is naked. Extending my apologies to

Mac Barnett for his brilliantly written book, I know I will never get through this story unless I do some extemporaneous editing.

"Blast that," shouted Taft.

"Perhaps," said Michelle Obama.

"That's right! Michele Obama is the First Lady of the United States of America," Sherri agrees.

"Uh Huh! The First Lady is Michelle Obama," echoes Donna.

In the end, to the satisfaction of Donna and Sherri, Michelle Obama finds a way to help President Taft get out of the bath. The rest of the class doesn't care who the First Lady is. They're too busy giggling over the naked president. The only unsatisfied student that day is Shane, the Taft scholar, who, rather disgusted, shows no appreciation for my editing skills, reminding me that Michelle Obama is *not* married to William Howard Taft. Then he storms off to check out a book on American presidential history to prove it.

4

Adventures in
Laughter and Tears

His eyes well up with tears because he forgot his library book and can't check out another one. This has become a habit, so I need to make a point that it is time to be responsible. At the same time, I not only want to be compassionate, I want to put books in the hands of readers. We librarians are protective of our collections. We don't think about the books belonging to the school. We think about them belonging to us. Though I want to be compassionate and make sure children have books, I look at this student with quivering lips and weepy eyes, and instead, think to myself about my budget and how many books this particular child has misplaced.

"There is no crying in the library," I tell him. "There is no crying in baseball, and there is no crying in the library!"

Truth is, there *is* crying in the library. Sometimes, they are tears of frustration when a tired first grader can't find the book he's been wanting for weeks. Sometimes they are tears of sadness when the girl a student wants to sit and read with prefers to sit with someone else. There are also tears when students make mistakes or even tears from me when a student I've been trying to reach lets me know through a kind word that I'm making progress with my students after all.

The tears I, myself, can't control are those that come when a former student returns after many years to share how I made a difference in her life, and even that after all these years, she remembers me. These are the tears that come when a parent stops by to report his child's college success and tells me, or other educators like me, that we are, in part, responsible for him becoming a teacher.

Then there are tears that come when I'm laughing so hard I don't have any choice but to let my tears flow. When laughter tears come, I can't breathe. I often let out a snort and have no ability to stop it. At first my students look at me like I'm crazy. Then before I know it, contagious giggle fits fill the room with laughing, snorting, crying students. Yes, there is no crying in baseball, but there are crying days in my library. Those days are good days.

Never A More Engaged Student

I begin this story with kindergartners sitting at my feet. I look at their smiling faces and shining eyes that tell me they are excited about my read-a-loud. One little boy stares at me with the most engaged expression.

Joey hangs on every word. His little face lights up with excitement and wonder. This, of course, inspires me to read with even more expression. I use silly voices and act out the story as I read. He sits at my feet, never moving or taking his eyes off me.

When the story is over, I ask if there are any questions. To my joy, this most engaged little boy raises his hand. I wait, excited for the question that I know will be filled with curiosity and wonder: "What's that stuff that jiggles on your neck when you're reading?" he asks.

From that day forward, I only wear turtlenecks.

As Kindergartners Wait in Line

I love overhearing the things kindergartners say while they wait in line to check out their library books.

"You don't have a book on peacocks?" says Jackie. "You mean I'm going to have to live with the books I have?"

"I told Trenton I loved him," says Natalie.

"Love is nice," I tell her. Natalie explains that it is better than nice and tells me that she is "in love" with Trenton.

"You're only 5, dear," I tell her. Once again, she explains that she is not 5. She is 6 years old, and Trenton is very cute. "That's good enough me for me!" she says.

While standing in line, Kathy points to the reading corner, telling me that Cameron is eating something off the floor. I ask him what he is doing.

"I found it on the floor. I didn't want to get up and throw it away, so I ate it."

"Really?" I ask, exasperated by his answer. "What is it?

"I don't know. It tasted like paper," he says.

Then Wendell looks at me with glowing eyes and a toothless grin: "I just love it when you call us your darlings."

Fractions

Math has never been my best subject. In fact, I can relate to the Facebook post I saw recently: "Another day passed, and I didn't use algebra once."

One day, a third grader asks me to help him with his paper on fractions. I tell him I'll take a look, but I haven't divided fractions since I was in the third grade.

"They had fractions when you were in the third grade?" Alan asks.

"Yes, my friend. That is the year they were invented."

Alan is impressed. "That's pretty cool. I know someone who was alive before fractions!"

I Believe I Can Fly

Out of breath, a third-grade girl runs up to my desk. Her face is flushed as she tells me that Chuck is singing a song with bad words. I look in his direction where he smiles at me and skips to my desk.

"What are you singing?" I ask.

In perfect pitch, he opens his mouth and sings, "I believe I can fly!" He holds the last note long and strong.

Janet, an expert in the lyrics of all songs, points out that there is more, and, she adds, "It's bad." The she folds her arms across her chest waiting for my reaction.

"I believe I can fly and what?" I ask.

At the top of his lungs, Chuck closes his eyes, waves his hands in the air, and belts out, "I believe I can fly. I want boobs that can touch the sky." All he's missing is a cell phone with a light to shine on the rest of his concert guests. Janet looks over at me with an *I told you it's bad* look. I wonder to myself, "Does he want a girl with boobs that can touch the sky, or does he want boobs for *himself* that can touch the sky?" Then my thoughts drift to "I wish I had boobs that touched the sky. At my age, they fall under my arm pits." Focus, Rhonda, focus! Bringing my attention back to Chuck and his impromptu concert, I ask if he is singing the song to Janet.

"No!" he answers, horrified. I ask Janet if he is singing to her. She replies with an equally adamant, "No!"

"He is singing it, and you overheard it. Is that correct?" I ask Janet.

"Yes," she says.

"You both need to know that there is nothing wrong with the word 'boobs.' If he were singing it to you Janet, then I would be concerned." I turn to Chuck and add, "Maybe you shouldn't sing in the library but focus on finding a good book to read." I turn to both of them and ask, "What does B. O. O. B. spell?

"Boob," Janet says, her cheeks flushing. With that, Chuck starts singing again right on key. "I believe I can fly. I want boobs that can touch the sky." I give him the "cut" signal, and he stops. "Yes. B.O.O.B. spells boob. "Now, I ask them, "What does B. O. O. K. spell?"

"Book!" they both answer. I tell them "book" is also correct. Then I tell them that since we're in the library, they need to forget the boobs and find a book!

I'm Going to Be Chubby

Brody is small for his age and can't seem to gain weight no matter what he eats. One morning he comes into the library and announces that they found a solution.

"Mrs. Eberst, I am going to be chubby," he says.

"Chubby?" I ask. Brody explains that he went to the doctor who gave him some new medicine so he could be chubby.

"You are going to look great," I say with a wink. "I take the same medicine!"

"Really?" he says, looking at me closely. "It works!"

Shared Tears

I feel blessed when I run into past students. Some I don't recognize at all; others have the same look they had when they were in elementary school. I'm humbled that they remember me.

Once I run into a very tall young man who asks me if I am a librarian. I tell him yes and ask if I should know him. He tells me his name and lets me know I had him in school a long time ago when he was a first grader. I tell him I remember the name, but suspect that he doesn't look anything like he did in first grade.

He says when he was in first grade, he had tears in his eyes every day. The only time the tears went away, he said, was when he came to the library. He remembers me reading to the class and making him laugh.

What a wonderful gift he gave me by sharing this memory. Now I have tears in *my* eyes.

You're A Better Librarian This Year

Vicki stops by the library the first week of school and informs me that I am a better librarian this year than I was last year. I thank her and ask, "What was wrong with me last year?"

"You weren't bad last year. You're just better this year. You let me check out harder books and your jokes are funnier," she says.

I'm glad to hear that my material is improving.

To Be Old Again

Ruby watches me intently as I am reading a book aloud. I look down at her and smile. She raises her hand quickly and asks me, "Do you wear dentures?" That isn't a question I'm expecting, so I reply, "No. Why do you ask?"

"All old people wear dentures," she answers, matter-of-factly.

Looking down at Ruby with less of a smile, I ask her, "How old do you think I am?"

"You've got to be at least 40."

I pat her on the head, smile, and go back to reading the story.

Oh, to be old again!

My Dad Drives a Vortex

My husband and I make a trip to Sedona, Arizona, over a long weekend. It's a well-earned getaway to see the red rocks and learn about the power of a vortex. The Sedona Chamber of Commerce Brochure reads: According to the scientific point of view, a vortex is an "area of enhanced linear energy flow." The energy of the vortex, says the local scientific community, is either "flowing upward out of the earth" or "flowing inward toward the earth." The scientific perspective proposes that "up flow vortexes boost spiritual energy and expansion of consciousness" while "in flow vortexes help one turn inward and enhance introspection."

I don't know if the Vortexes I visit are up flow or in flow, and don't really care because three days in the Arizona sun not only turned my skin the color of the rocks, it did, indeed, expand my consciousness and enhance my introspection. I came back to school relaxed, full of compassion and love, ready to be forgiving of overdue library books.

But Sally loses more than one book this year. I am always troubled by this, yet at the same time, every student needs a book to read. Though my budget doesn't allow me to replace every lost book, I do feel the need to help students like Sally learn to be responsible for them. Sometimes students check out a book in their teacher's name and leave the book in the teacher's classroom. Other times, they just lose the book somewhere at home. Often, I will just gather paperbacks that are much easier to replace.

"It's been a long time since you checked out a book," I say to Sally. "You can't find the book that's missing?" She tells me she's looked everywhere for it but can't find it. She looks sad when she tells me her parents don't have the money to pay for the book. I instantly feel bad for her, knowing that she has no control over the financial situation of her family.

"I think you need to check out a book," I say. "I'll make you a deal. You come in at recess tomorrow and work with me for half an hour, and I'll remove the book from your record."

She looks at me with a smile. Then, like she wants to cry. "I'll do that! After that, can I really check out a book?"

"Yes," I tell her. "And you'll be taking responsibility for the missing book by working off your debt." I also tell her this is a onetime deal. She has to come up with a plan in the future so she won't lose another book. She smiles again and tells me that she can't believe I would do this for her.

"That's what happens when Mrs. Eberst goes to Sedona, Arizona and sits on a vortex in the red rocks and stares at the scenery for a few days. See you at recess!"

Sally looks up at me, not sure about what I just said. Then suddenly, she understands: "My dad drives a Vortex!"

The Cleveland Browns

Chip and Danny can always be found in the sports section when their first-grade class comes to the library. Neither one cares about reading anything but books about football. In truth, neither one of them can read the books they are looking at, but it doesn't matter to them. As long as the man on the cover is wearing pads, a helmet, and a colorful jersey, they don't really care if the words make sense.

One day, their heated conversation about the Cleveland Browns draws me toward them. Danny sees me coming and tells me that Chip stole his book on the Browns. I look at the book the boys are arguing over and see that it's about the Denver Broncos and not the Cleveland Browns.

"This book is not about the Browns but the Broncos. Both teams start with the letter 'B.'" Then, throwing in a quick phonics lesson, I ask, "Can you tell me what the letter 'B' sounds like?"

"B.b.b.b.b. Browns," Chip says.

"That is correct. The title on this book is not Browns. It is Broncos." Danny holds up another book and asks if this book is about the Browns. "No, this book is about the Patriots. See, it starts with a 'P' not a 'B.'" Danny is frustrated and looks at the book about the Patriots.

"Is it okay if I pretend it's about the Browns?" he asks, hugging his book.

"Pretend away, my friend!" I tell him as he runs to my desk, telling everyone he is reading a book about his favorite team. I watch his excitement and think to myself, "Everyone in Ohio pretends any winning team is the Browns."

We Called Them Girlfriends

Kellie, a first grader, runs over to me in the library and says that the boys are saying bad things about the girls. My first thought is they stayed up and watched the 2016 Republican Presidential Debate on television the night before.

I walk over to the boys and ask them what they are saying about the girls. I explain that the girls are upset, so I'm concerned.

Greg, who could never be dishonest, quietly says, "We are calling them…" He takes a long pause and then looking ashamed says, "We are calling them girlfriends."

Robbie can't believe Greg has admitted to what they've been doing. He feels betrayed, looks at Greg, and shouts, "What did you say that for?"

Greg, the future Boy Scout, simply says, "She asked."

I explain to them both that there is nothing wrong with the word "girlfriend," but as first graders, "You are much too young to have girlfriends." Trying to cover the true intent of their conversation, Robbie tells me he is talking about his mom.

"Your mom is your girlfriend?" I ask. It must not have sounded the same when I say it. "No, that would be gross!"

Ever the Boy Scout, Greg puts on a love-struck smile and says, "My mom is my girlfriend!"

"That is lovely." Then I smile back, telling them that mothers love being their first-grade sons' girlfriends. Taking the opportunity to give some motherly advice, I say, "Now both of you promise me that whenever you talk about a girl, you will say only nice things. Never say anything bad or unkind."

"Every time?" Robbie asks.

"Every time."

"Do you mean *all* girls?"

"All girls," I say. "Get it?"

Robbie rolls his eyes and looks around the room at all the girls. Meanwhile, Greg makes the sign of the Boy Scout promise and commits to being nice to all girls—at least while he's in the library.

The Lost Library Book

Jim is always coming to class without his library books. He has a collection of unlimited excuses that range from "my mother forgot to put it in my book bag" to which I reply I don't recall his mother coming to the library to check out the book to "I think it's on the bookshelf in my bedroom." Each week Jim rolls his eyes, pretending to be annoyed at my question. He answers the same question week after week. The look on his face says it all: "Why are you asking the same question every week when you already know the answer?"

One morning before class Jim comes running in to the library, grinning from ear to ear and shouting that he found his library books. Since I had been nagging him for weeks, I am relieved. Throwing my hands in the air, I say, "Fabulous!"

"Be careful," he cautions, "they might still be cold."

"Why are they cold?" I ask.

"Well, I couldn't find them because my little brother put them in the refrigerator."

"How did you find them?" I ask with great interest.

"I went for a snack," he says, matter-of-fact.

Turn Left at Starbucks

I have a very sarcastic sense of humor, and most of the time students aren't sure if I'm serious or being clever. On more than one occasion, their teacher has had to explain that Mrs. Eberst is just joking.

Tom, Scott, and Ken come into the library one day looking for the papers they sent to my printer. I ask them if they know where the printer is. "No," they reply.

I tell them to go back to the main hall, turn left, go out the door, and walk across the walkway to the high school. "Once you are in the high school, take a left in the main hall, and then a quick right," I tell them. "Then walk to the front door and continue walking until you get to Summit Road."

I continue my directions, clearly and quickly. They listen, trying to remember what I'm telling them. "Stay on Summit until you reach Broad Street. You will come upon a group of businesses. Take a left at Starbucks." I ask them if they know where Starbucks is on Broad Street. They nod their heads "yes."

"Cross the parking lot to Subway and pick up a turkey sandwich for me. Don't forget to have it toasted. After you get the sandwich, turn around and re-track your steps to Broad Street, then to Summit, and through the high school all the way to the entrance to our school where, once inside, you know the way back to the library. Once you drop the sandwich off at my desk, walk into the back room of the library and get your papers. Do you want me to write this down for you?" I ask.

The three boys stare at me with that look I've seen many times. They're not sure if I'm serious or not. Over the years, some students take everything literally and do anything I ask not to disappoint me, while others laugh at everything I say. They are the students who have been around long enough to know how I am.

Scott is thinking out loud and says, "So, we turn left at the end of the hall?" After the look Tom gives him, it strikes Scott that I am not serious. To make sure he asks, "You're joking, right?"

"I think she's joking," says Tom, who has inherited my sarcasm after knowing me since kindergarten. He tells me I crack him up.

"The printer is in the back. Go," I tell them. As they leave the library, Ken, who is new to the building, is very quiet during this entire exchange. He tells his new friends, "I can't believe she had the nerve to ask us to leave school to get her a sandwich."

You Would Know If You'd Been Kissed

Blake is popular with the students in his kindergarten class. All the boys gravitate toward him because they want to be like him. It's probably because he knows the names of all the Power Rangers, Star Wars characters, and can burp the alphabet. It's not quite what he needs to know about the ABC's for kindergarten, but for other five-year-old boys, Blake is the perfect role model. The girls are oblivious to his charms except for one, Christine, who, by kindergarten standards, is a woman of the world. She can read and recognize talent when she sees it, as she smiles with glee when Blake shares the alphabet, something he can do at the drop of a hat and without the aid of a carbonated beverage. Blake, however, is a little slow when it comes to the women in the kindergarten world.

"I just kissed Blake on the lips," Christine announces.

"Really? Did you really kiss him on the lips?" I ask. She gives me a sly smile, batting her eyelashes. I look at Blake, "Did she kiss you on the lips?"

"I don't know," Blake says.

"You don't know? You don't know if a girl kissed you on the lips?"

"Uh, no," he says.

I ask Christine what she did. She closes her eyes tight, puckers her lips, and lets her head rotate around in circles making an "mmmmmm" sound. By her demonstration, there isn't a boy alive who wouldn't know he had been kissed on the lips—except maybe Blake. His passions are limited to burping sounds and superheroes.

Jeremiah the Bullfrog

A handsome high school junior walks up to me and asks, "Are you Mrs. Eberst?" This happens often. Then former students will share tales with me of my Converse shoes or the silly hats they remember. Jeremiah has another memory. I look at him and recognize that I should know him. "I had you at Slate Ridge, right?" Then I apologize that I don't remember his name. Without hesitating, Jeremiah sings out loud and strong, "Bom, Bom, Bom!" Instantly, I remember him and join in: "Jeremiah was a bullfrog. BOM, BOM, BOM!"

Together, with arms raised, we dance as we sing the chorus of the song. His friend looks at us both like we have totally lost our minds.

"You sang that to me every time you saw me for two years," he says, looking pleased.

"Yes, sir, I did."

As I try to hold back my emotions, Jeremiah looks at me, puts his arm around me, and says, "I loved it." With a lump in my throat, I tell him, "I did, too."

5

Adventures in
Testing the Waters

There is something about elementary children, especially boys, finding great joy in being inappropriate. They love to say things they are sure will shock you. After a group of third graders have a questionable conversation at lunch, for example, a student tells me he can't explain what they said because, "It is bad, and you won't be able to handle it." I tell him I appreciate the warning but explain that if I can't handle it, then maybe they shouldn't talk about it. Adults who think they can handle the topics of such lunchroom conversation might want to check out any episode of *Family Guy* to understand exactly what kids talk about among themselves.

Elementary school children especially test the waters of appropriateness. They speak openly about body parts and bodily functions. At 8 years old, these words are exciting to say, so students show no interest in learning when or when *not* to use such words in conversation. Boys frequently discuss body parts, mostly their own, and if their female classmates overhear them, they act oblivious as to why the girls are offended.

Young students gasp with delight when a classmate uses profanity, laughing with the boy who shares the new vocabulary word. Then they repeat the word, even if in a whisper, just to see what it feels like to say the word. Though they, themselves, swear in secret, they also relish any opportunity to tattle on their friend for swearing.

Often, whenever young students disagree with me about something I do or say that they don't like, they will refuse to let go of their discontent, misunderstanding my direction to "drop it," and thinking, instead, that I mean to say, "repeat it again." This is how elementary students test the waters to see how far they can push me or a classmate in a disagreement. They will even testify, as if under oath, that they didn't do it, even when I witness the disagreement myself. I've learned that most of the time when a student is testing the waters in any situation, they are slyly looking at me out of the corner of their eye while they're doing or saying what is inappropriate.

Warning: an adult may find some of the things in this chapter inappropriate. Ten year-olds, on the other hand, find them shockingly funny and entertaining.

Can You Say Mammal?

A group of fourth grade boys with animated expressions huddle around a book. Every once in a while, they look up and scout the library to see if anyone is watching them. When it looks like the coast is clear, they turn their attention back to the book. I hear whispers and walk closer to listen.

"It's kind of gross," says Kent.

"I don't think it is appropriate for school," says Charlie. Just then, Carl walks by and asks to see. "Whoa!" he says, not taking his eyes off the book.

"Nice," Jim adds.

I walk over to the group of boys. As I'm about to ask what they're looking at, Jim quickly shuts the book. I see the cover with the title, *Food*. Pulling the book from the clutches of Jim's grip, I ask, "What are you looking at? You seem awfully interested." I get a variety of answers but with downcast eyes. Only Joe confesses.

"Dirty pictures," he whispers, looking around at the other boys who return a look of disgust. I open to the dog-eared page and see a photograph of a nursing mother. Not just a mother holding her infant in the position to nurse, but one that would cause the Anti-Breast Feeding in Public Coalition to cringe. The photo could have been used as a "How to attach a child to nipple" example in the La Leche League training brochure.

"This is not a dirty picture," I say casually. "Do you know why women have breasts?" The boys faces turn red. Whatever they're thinking it's obviously not the answer I'm looking for. I ask again if they know why women have breasts.

Jim bravely answers, "Yes."

"Why do women have breasts, Jim?" I ask.

Kent looks at Jim with amazement and quickly asks, "Why?"

All eyes are on Jim. His friends wait with bated breath for the answer.

"I'm not saying it in front of Mrs. Eberst," he says.

Carl leans in and under his breath, whispers to Jim to tell him. Jim uncomfortably tells Carl to shut up.

"Really? You're using the 'S' word at a time like this?" I say. I open the book, hold up the picture of the nursing mother and ask one more time why women have breasts.

"I'm not going to answer that because I'll get in trouble," Jim says. I tell him not in my class he won't. His face turns a deeper red while his friends stand around him, anxious for the answer. He shamefully admits that he doesn't know. The disappointment of his friends is audible. They turn to me for the answer.

I close the book and look at each one of them. They don't move. They don't say a word. I can feel them lean in closer to me as I begin to speak.

"Can you say mammal?" I ask. Their faces are blank. "Look it up," I tell them, taking the book. They stand in their huddle, confused and disappointed.

The story of the food book travels quickly throughout the school. It makes its way down to the third grade where two boys run into the library and ask where I keep the books on food. I suspiciously ask if they have a specific food in mind.

"The one the fourth-grade boys are all talking about," they ask, wide-eyed.

That afternoon a teacher stops by the library after lunch duty and tells me that a group of third-grade boys asked her how you feed a baby.

I'm glad to hear that the fourth-grade boys took my advice and looked it up.

It Hurts When You Get
Hit in the Nibble

I'm a fairly patient person. I don't expect silence in the library. I tell the students that if they are too quiet, I'm concerned about what they're doing. Exploring the library is not a quiet venture, so I tell them that I should be able to hear learning. However, after fifteen minutes of constant tattling and whining that someone "won't be my friend" (conversations not in my definition of learning), I sentence the entire class to silent reading.

Suddenly, Sam, a first grader, runs to my desk with a horrified look. Brad, another first grader, is not far behind with an equally mortified look.

"Brad says someone threw a ball at him, and it hit his nipple," says Sam.

"No, it didn't," Brad says, making sure I know he would never say such an offensive word as nipple. "I said 'nibble.'"

Knowing full well that Brad *would* say such an offensive word, I tell him that a nipple is a part of our body. "Now go back and read your book."

Not satisfied with my lack of compassion for his traumatic experience, Brad pleads with me, "But someone threw a ball and hit me in my nibble!"

Now I'm beginning to show signs of *this is not the conversation Mrs. Eberst wants to be having with you.* I humor Brad anyway and ask him, "What is a nibble?"

Sam speaks up, explaining to me what Brad is really trying to say, hoping to avoid what he thinks will be a scolding about inappropriate words.

"He meant nibble. Like you are going to nibble on an apple." I had to give him credit. For a first grader, that's not a bad use of the word, even though it is totally out of context.

"No! That is not what nibble means," Brad says, correcting Sam. "I got hit in the nibble." He then points downward below his belt. For the first time, Sam understands what Brad is telling him. With a look of relatable horror, Sam holds up his finger and thumb about an inch apart, and asks, "You mean your little nibble?"

At this point, my patience is wearing thin. I tell them to sit down and read a book.

Brad looks at me hurt that I'm not sympathetic to the seriousness of his story about getting hit in the nibble. "But it hurts to get hit in the nibble," he repeats.

"Brad," I say as calmly as I can. "It hurts when you use the word 'nibble.' Go read your book!"

Freak

Third grade boys are not always nice to each other. Even friends get picky with one another for no reason but to pick. They don't have to be mad at each other to have words and attitudes rise to the surface, especially when it's the last period of the day after a long week of school. When under the influence of "it's almost the weekend," they have very little ability to think and act rationally.

"He called me a freak!" Brad tattles while waiting in line.

Michael steps in front of him, posturing for an argument, "I did not!" I know they have a history and do my best to keep them apart. "Michael," I ask. "Why did you call him a freak?"

He steps back, looks me in the eye, and says, "I didn't, even though he *is* singing a stupid song."

"Not as stupid as you are," Brad shouts with his chest puffed up.

My patience is limited as I, too, am under the influence of "it's almost the weekend." "Really? You know better than to act like that. Is this how you two are going to talk to each other?" I scold. They both respond with a yes. "No!" I say. "Michael, what did you call him?"

Knowing that he has pushed me a bit too far, Michael choses his words carefully. "I uhhh. I uhhh called him an Eek."

"Is that right? You expect me to buy that?" I say. "What is it? Dr. Seuss Insult Day?

Brad raises his hand and with a smile says that he likes Dr. Seuss. I give him a look. He stops talking. Michael puts his head down, pretending to be humble and says, "I really did call him an Eek."

"He did not. He called me a freak," shouts Brad.

"Michael, do you expect me to believe that?" I ask. "Do you think I'm that naïve?"

"I don't know what that means," he says.

"You can look it up when we're finished here. Now apologize."

Michael looks at me and says he is sorry. "Not to me, to him!" I say, pointing to Brad. Michael looks at Brad in disgust. Then he looks at me. "What for?"

"For calling him an Eek!" I say.

"I didn't call him an Eek. I called him a freak." Michael stops himself before he says any more, turns to Brad and says, "I'm sorry." They walk to a table together, and I smile . . . rather pleased with myself.

He's in High School Now

A first grader has been missing from class a few days when I ask if anyone knows where he is. Spencer, who knows everything, fills me in on his friend, telling me that Jake doesn't go to school here anymore.

"He's in high school now," says Spencer.

"That's very interesting," I say. "But I don't think you can be in first grade one day and in high school the next."

"I saw him after school," Spencer explains. "He says he's in 'high school' now."

Correcting his friend, Steve tells us that Jake isn't in high school. "He showed his middle finger to the teacher, and Spencer knows that's true because he saw it himself."

"He gets a few days off of school!" Steve testifies.

Spencer thinks for a minute and says, "I told you. He's in high school now. That's what they do in high school."

It Is Inappropriate!

Teni and David are best friends. On one hand, both first graders could be mistaken for characters on the *Big Bang Theory*. On the other, their six-year-old social IQ doesn't even come close to average, let alone that of their advancing brains. On this particular day, they're fighting when they get off the bus, which is unusual for the friends. I have witnessed them debate about a scientific theory or argue about a math equation, but I've never seen them fight like they're fighting today.

Teni is holding a sheet of ripped and crumpled paper. With tears in his eyes, he tells me that David ripped the page. David jumps in to explain his behavior: "He wrote something inappropriate, and so I ripped it up!" I let David know that if there's a problem, then he should get a teacher for help instead of dealing with it himself.

"But it is inappropriate!" he repeats rather dramatically.

"It doesn't matter," I say. "You need to get a teacher when there's a problem with another student. It isn't your job to discipline someone else. Ripping Teni's paper is wrong."

"The paper is in. a. pro. pri. ate," he says, emphasizing each syllable as he speaks.

"Ripping someone's paper is inappropriate!" I say, bending down and putting my face close to his to illustrate how stern I feel at this moment.

Matching my gaze, David begins," Innappro…"

"Do not speak!" I say firmly.

Standing certain in his assessment about what is right and wrong, David bravely finishes his statement. "priate!" he says. I don't have to speak. By the expression on my face, he knows exactly what I am going to say. He closes his lips tight, and I think for a moment that his social IQ is suddenly higher than I once thought since he's showing good social judgment not to answer back. I put my arm out, point to the building. "Tell Teni you are sorry and then go to class!"

David looks at his friend and quickly says he's sorry. As someone who must always have the last word, however, he looks over his shoulder and quickly insists, "It is inappropriate." After one more look at me, he turns to follow the crowd into the building.

I put my hand on Teni's shoulder, as he looks at the crumpled paper in his hands.

"Let me see it," I ask. He looks up at me with sad eyes, sheepishly handing me the page. Teni's shoulders slump, and his head falls as he looks down at the sidewalk. I take the student- disciplined paper and open it carefully. In scratched, first-grade penmanship I read:

"Someday, I am going to marry Miss Piggy." The written words are followed by a big red heart.

"The Muppet?" I ask. Looking up at me with sparkling eyes and a huge toothless grin, he breathlessly whispers, "Yes." I smooth out the crumpled paper the best I can and fold it neatly. Handing the love note back to him, I say, "I want you to promise me you will keep this paper in your book bag. Then take it home and put it in a place where you keep all your treasures. Keep it safe. When you are older, you will understand."

We walk together toward the building. David is waiting for us with his face pressed against the window. As we walk by him, he reminds us through the glass how he feels about the note and mouths, again, that it is inappropriate.

I put my face up to the glass and mouth back, "Go to class!"

Opening the door to the building, I look at Teni's face. He is filled with joy. As I watch him run to class, I think to myself that every girl should have a boy who looks like that when he thinks about her.

It Is Art

While exploring the shelves to find something new to read, Brian finds a book in the art section that contains a photo of a sculpture of a naked Colossus. He immediately runs to my desk talking about something "bad" in his book.

"It is a sculpture of Colossus. It isn't bad. It's art," I say calmly.

He seems okay with the answer and walks away. I watch him as he shows the picture to other students. The boys giggle and a few girls say, "That's gross." After I watch Brian make the rounds to his classmates, I call him over.

"I see that you're sharing your library book. That is excellent," I tell him as I take the book and open the cover to the worn page. Pointing to the picture of Colossus, I ask, "What are you telling them when you show them this picture?"

Brian hesitates. "I tell them . . . well . . . I tell them it's funny."

"And?" I look at him, waiting for his answer. Unable to make eye contact with me, Brian looks down and says, "Don't make me tell you."

"Tell me," I whisper.

"Fine!" he says, giving in, knowing I won't let it go. "I told them to look at his penis. It is funny." I knew that was coming when I sent him off to read the book. "What did I tell you about the picture when you first showed it to me?" I ask. Rolling his eyes, Brian says, "It is a sculpture of Colosssooooosuuuuss."

"Colossus. It is art," I say clearly. "Now, what are you going to tell your friends when you share your book?"

He tells me rather unconvincingly, "It is art."

"Yes, it is ART," I repeat. Under his breath, Brian mumbles, "But look at his penis."

"It's art, Brian. Art," I say again. With all the courage he can muster, Brian tells me, "It's a penis."

"Art!" I repeat again. When Brian tries to share his assessment of the photo, I give him the "don't speak" look. Without saying a word, he mouths the word "penis." With the same dramatic intent, I silently mouth the word "art" and point to the table where he sits.

The truth is it looks more like a mustache than a penis, as I remind myself that it is art.

Lost Cell Phone

A colleague of mine found a cell phone in the street between the high school and the elementary school. It was probably dropped by a high school student running to catch his bus. Turning it on, I look to see if there are any clues to its rightful owner. Of course the phone has a security code, but I can see the screen saver picture. If the student who lost this phone wants to prove his ownership, he will need to answer the following questions:

1. Please describe the screen saver picture. No detail should be left out. I am interested in your choice of photos. Since you are only in high school, I'd also like an explanation.

2. Please look me in the eye and tell me the name of the lovely high school girl wearing the leopard thong with matching push-up bra and pouting provocatively at the camera while taking this selfie? She is lovely, but she'd be a real knockout in a cute black dress with matching heels, smiling ever so sweetly to enhance her character and heighten her virtue.

3. Have you shown this picture to your mother? (When you first introduce this girl to your mother, make sure she's not wearing the leopard outfit. Have her put on the cute black dress with matching heels instead. Don't forget the virtuous smile.)

4. Have you shown this picture to her father? (When you do, I hope you're on the track team and that you move quickly.)

Thank you for dropping your phone at a time when one of our elementary students did not find it. If you can answer all the above questions to my satisfaction, then you may have your phone back.

Like a Good Woman Should

Since we are a STEM school, we celebrate a bit differently than your standard holiday celebrations. Every October, instead of dressing for Halloween, we hold a parade for the high school where all our students dress in their STEM costumes. Some students represent the sciences in some form, while others show their technology, engineering, or math creativity. We've had students dressed like Math Facts, Cell Phones, and teachers.

It is a great honor for me when Isaac dresses like the librarian. His costume is complete with a red wig, glasses, and a sweater. He tops it all off by borrowing my extra staff ID, proudly announcing, "I am Mrs. Eberst!"

Weeks before this event, we brainstorm and go to the design cycle to figure out what costume would be creative and best represent Science, Technology, Engineering, and Math. As we discuss this, I must explain that a vampire dressed like a doctor, though creative, doesn't quite fit the constraints of the challenge.

As we discuss the challenge and what each student might wear to the parade, I notice Johnny is looking down at his feet and not participating in the conversation. I know he doesn't celebrate holidays and think that he might be confused about the intent of our assignment. His parents have strong feelings about holidays celebrated in the public schools and which books are in the library.

Johnny tries hard to fit in and often struggles between what he knows his parents would approve of and what other kids are doing. I want to be mindful of this when I choose my words so when he goes home to tell his parents, they aren't confused or concerned.

I'm already not their favorite person since I know they asked the principal about whether I was teaching witchcraft and wizardry because I had Harry Potter on the bookshelves. I'm thankful they didn't see the voodoo doll of the superintendent on my desk that a union member gave me when I was negotiating our contract. Finally, it's sealed that I am not their favorite teacher when they hear that each year I make up a silly oath, asking that students promise not to eat peanut butter, marshmallow and dill pickle sandwiches while reading their library books AND that they promise to bring back what they borrow on the date due. Johnny refuses to raise his hand for the promise, saying that his parents told him to never take an oath with Mrs. Eberst.

So I choose my words carefully, not to offend or be misrepresented to mom and dad, but to make Johnny feel he can join in the fun of STEM day without compromise: "Remember, students, we are not celebrating Halloween. We are celebrating STEM. You can dress as anything you want: a plant, a math fact, or even a famous scientist. There are a lot of careers in STEM you could represent." Johnny looks up at me with interest.

"What kind of costumes could you wear?" he asks.

Students begin to shout out what they are wearing or the person they might dress up as. Tommy shares that he is going to dress up as his dad because he's an engineer. "That's a great idea!" I say. "What does your dad do for a job, Johnny?" He snips at me and tells me his dad "got laid off and doesn't do anything." This isn't starting off as well as I had hoped it would.

"What kind of work does your mother do?" I ask.

Johnny looks at me, stands up rather dramatically, and wags his finger at me, proclaiming, "She stays home like a good woman should!"

This Is Not Your Library Book

Amy has been missing her library book for a few weeks. I watch her walk to the stacks and pull another copy of the book she checked out and bring it to my desk, telling me she found the book she needed to return. I scan the book knowing that this isn't the copy she checked out.

"This isn't the copy you checked out Amy. I have several copies of the same title, and this is not yours." She insists that she walked into the library holding this book. She says she is returning it now, and I need to take it off her record. I show her the barcode with the number for the book and the number on the computer. "They aren't the same book," I say.

"You have made a mistake Mrs. Eberst. This is my book and you need to take it off my record," she says abruptly.

I tell her that when she returns the book that is checked out to her, I will take it off her record. After I say this, she takes a deep breath, tilts her chin up in the air, and closes her eyes. Very slowly, she raises her arm and stretches her fingers apart pointing them at me. Then she begins to hum. After a minute, she stops and lowers her hand to her side. She opens her eyes, looks at me with a satisfied expression, and walks out of the library without a word.

I never get the book back, but her teacher explains to me that this student practices voodoo. I'm not sure if she practices for real, but now I've seen how she uses voodoo when she's missing her library books and her homework. This does explain why, however, from that day forward, I developed a tick each time a student is missing a book.

First Grade Vocabulary Lesson

The best part of lunch duty is walking around and listening to conversations. While I am cutting open ketchup packets, a first grader says, "Mrs. Eberst, he called me sexy." I look at Jeff who defiantly tells me that he did not. I ask him if "sexy" is a good word to use in the cafeteria.

"It isn't a bad word," he tells me.

"You're right. It isn't a bad word," I agree. "It isn't a first-grade word either."

Jeff tells me okay and asks, "What is a first-grade word?"

I think for a minute, putting my finger on my chin, and looking up. "Hmmm," I say. "How about 'burp' and 'fart.' Now those are first grade words. I hear them all the time from first graders." Students at the table burst out laughing and agree that "burp" and "fart" are better words than "sexy."

I smile to myself, thinking how much trouble I'm now in with the first-grade teachers.

Putting New Words in My Mouth

Daron is our self-appointed class censor. He hears words and reports those that are good to use in kindergarten and those that are not. One day Daron marches up to my desk and tells me that Spencer swore. Most kindergartners don't know that some words have more than one meaning. For example, Daron falls apart the day a student checks out a book on the Hoover Dam. He wants to know why I would allow a book about swear words in the library. Another time, he finds a book with the call number E SEX. He cannot understand my explanation that SEX is the first three letters of the author's name.

When Daron's classmate Spencer actually *says* a swear word, Daron is beside himself and shares with me the swear word he heard with his ears uttered by his friend. I ask Spencer to come behind my desk so we can have some privacy. I take his hands in mine and ask him what he said. He says, "Jesus Christ!" in just the way you would expect to hear him say this name if he were swearing. However, in the past, I've had students testify to others using these words. I wasn't sure about how Spencer was actually using the words, so I tell him, "Daron says you were swearing. Can you tell me why you said what you did?" I am hoping he will tell me that he was praying. Instead, he states rather boldly, "I saw something in his book that I didn't like, so I said, 'Jesus Christ!'"

I sit back for a moment and look at Spencer. "When you say that word in the way you did, it is offensive to people who believe in Jesus."

He tells me that he believes in Jesus. He looks at me for a moment, and I can see the wheels turning in his head. Then it suddenly dawns on him: "Is that his name?" Sounding astonished, Spencer asks me, "You mean Jesus is his first name and Christ is his last name?" He can't believe his discovery. Correcting himself, he explains his behavior. "Jesus was not in my head when I said Jesus Christ."

"No, sweetie. I didn't think He was. You should find new words to put in your head.

Spencer wants to know why we need to put new words in our head.

"We use words to tell how we feel or what we think about," I explain. "The words we have in our head are important because what is in our head comes out of our mouth. If we put the right words in, we don't even have to think about them before we say them."

"Do you want me to put new words in my head?" he asks.

"Yes," I tell him. "You can do what I do and find new words to put in your head to use when you're shocked or surprised. Like the word 'Whoa!'"

"Like, holy shit?" Spencer asks. I tell him that we need to find other words that would be better to put in our heads. Then I send him back to his book because at that moment, I have no new words in my head to respond to his new words, except maybe, "Whoa!"

That's Probably Not a Good Idea

I watch with interest as Zac, a kindergartner, works the circulation desk. He is a master at charming female patrons. In fact, he's a natural—the way he smiles and then looks past them, pretending to ignore their giggles. That's not something you can learn in kindergarten. He's even suave the way he holds their library books, scans the barcodes, and tells them to have a nice day. To be honest, I think it's a gift he was born with.

Not until Taylor hands her books to him to be checked out do I discover just how debonair Zac really is. "He likes me," Taylor tells me, pointing to Zac. "He tried to kiss me." I look at Zac, who shrugs his shoulders like it's no big deal. Taylor continues telling me that he kissed her hand.

"That is very gentlemanly of you," I say, looking at him. Zac smiles at me. Taylor smiles at me. Then they smile at each other.

Nonchalantly she says, "He also picks his nose and eats his boogers." I look at Zac, who shrugs his shoulders again like it's no big deal.

"Let me get this straight, Taylor. You let Zac kiss your hand after he picks his nose and eats his boogers?" She stares at Zac. He raises his eyebrows and smiles at her. Taylor thinks about this for a minute, then she says to me, "That's probably not a good idea. Right?"

"Right," I tell her. "You shouldn't let a boy kiss you just because he smiles at you." I remind her she is only in kindergarten and that she should be a little older and a little more selective when a boy wants to kiss her.

I turn to Zac. "It's probably not a good idea, buddy, to pick your nose, eat your boogers, and expect a girl to let you kiss her hand." He smiles, then confidently shrugs his shoulders like it's no big deal.

She Said The "H" Word

Carissa tells me that Marla used the "h" word. I'm not sure which "h" word she is talking about, so I ask her to whisper it in my ear, assuring her she won't be in trouble for saying it.

She can hardly get the word out. Finally, after hesitating, she whispers, "Hell." I thank her for the information and send her on her way. Then I call Marla to my desk and ask her what word she is using that maybe she shouldn't be using. Most students tell me they didn't say anything, some change the word, but Marla is very sure of the word she says.

"Hell," she admits boldly.

"Tell me what you said to Carissa," I ask, wanting to know what context she used the word.

Marla tells me that she isn't swearing. "I told her that if she isn't quiet in the library and doing what she is supposed to do, she will go to hell." Then Marla continues her sermon. "If you don't do the right thing, you will end up in hell."

I tell her I am glad she isn't swearing. "However, even though you are not swearing, 'Hell' is probably not the best thing to say," I advise her.

"Well, if she isn't careful, she is going to go to hell!" she warns.

"I will certainly tell her that she needs to be careful," I promise. Then I add, "Please don't tell others they are going to go to hell in the library. OK?"

"OK," she says.

I think about this for a while and wonder if using the "h" word would inspire some students to bring back their library books on time.

Do I Look Like Your Mother?

Each morning students carry in crates of library books to be checked in before their class arrives. I require that the students take the books out of the crate, put them on my desk in stacks of chapter books, nonfiction, and easy fiction. Not only does this help me speed up the process, but it's a good exercise for the students to know the different categories of books available in the library.

On this day, two fourth graders drop a crate of books off at my desk and begin to walk away, so I call them back: "You know the drill. You unload the crate by chapter books, non-fiction, and easy fiction. That's your job. You just dumped a pile of books on my desk for me to clean up. Not only did you leave more work for me, but more importantly, you missed out on a chance to practice reading call numbers and separating books. I'm not cleaning up your mess. Do I look like your mother?"

They stare at me for a second. Then with a sly grin, Jerry says, "No. Maybe more like my grandmother." Pete, who is helping him with the book returns, suddenly has a look of horror on his face. He can't believe the gall of his friend. Sheepishly, Jerry looks at me to see how I will respond.

Pretending to be offended I say, "Excuse me?"

"Okay, Okay. You look more like my mother," Jerry says.

Before I can tell Jerry that it would be wise to never make that mistake again, Pete, still in shock, looks at his friend and in a half whisper tells him, "You better tell her she looks more like your older sister." Pete is wise beyond his years.

The Spitter

Ohio takes football seriously. There is nothing more insulting than making a disparaging remark about the Buckeyes, especially if the remark comes from a Michigan fan.

Dan, wearing a maize-and-blue shirt says, "Mrs. Eberst, he spit on me." Looking at the accused spatter and thinking this is out of character for this student, I call him over and ask what happened.

Paul, wearing scarlet and gray, proudly declares that Dan made him mad. So I ask Dan to tell me what happened. "I told him Ohio State sucked," Dan explains, "and if he didn't cheer for Michigan, he was stupid."

I think to myself that if he said that to me, I would have spit on him, too, but remembering I am the adult in the room, I ask, "Can you think of words to say other than 'suck' or 'stupid' to express what you want to say?

He gives me an annoyed, "Yes."

"So, let me make sure I understand what happened. You said what you said and Paul spit on you?"

"Yes, sort of."

"Sort of?" I ask.

"What does that mean?"

Talking fast, Dan begins trying to explain. "I said Ohio State sucked . . . I mean, aren't very good and that he was stu. . . not smart. Then he blew a raspberry."

I look at Dan. "A raspberry? He didn't spit, but blew a raspberry?" Dan glares at Paul and says, "Yes." I point to the stacks and tell Dan to go find a library book and think about how he could have better handled this. When he walks away, I put my arm around Paul. Then in a voice of guidance and reason, I tell him, "Maybe, it's not a good idea to blow a raspberry in someone's face just because they insult your team. He's wrong about the Buckeyes, though, and we both know it. No more blowing raspberries in the library. Thank you for not spitting."

Then we give each other a high five and a hearty "Go Bucks!"

The "P" Word

I love it when third graders think they say things that shock you. They learn quickly that their teachers have been around long enough that it takes a lot to make us cringe. It doesn't take much time in my class to know that nothing surprises me.

Judy shyly walks over to my desk, leans down, and whispers in my ear. "Mrs. Eberst," she says, pointing to a group of boys. "They said an inappropriate word." I always love it when a student tells me they heard or saw something inappropriate. It usually means someone said the "s" word, which turns out to be "stupid" or "shut up." We used different inappropriate "s" words when I was a kid. Still standing next to me, Judy continues to whisper, "It is an inappropriate boy part."

Now, I'm intrigued. I wonder what body part she thinks is inappropriate. To third graders, it could by anything. I tell her thank you and that I will talk to them. All I have to do is look up from my desk since the boys are watching intently as Judy whispers in my ear. I point to Jon who, with his head down, walks to my desk.

He takes a deep breath, a sure sign of guilt in my experience. "So, Junior, which inappropriate word are you using today?" Jon won't look at me when he answers. "I can't say."

"Come on," I goad him. You are comfortable enough to say it to the girls. I'm a girl. Tell me." He looks up at me, and in his defense, says that they aren't saying it to the girls, but the girls just overheard it.

"What did they overhear?" I ask.

Jon looks at the floor, takes a deep breath. "The 'p' word," he says.

"The 'p' word?" I ask. He looks up at me. "You know . . . ." He points down.

I've been an expert in prepubescent sign language for a long time. I know the word and so I say, "Penis?"

Jon takes a step back and shuffles his feet uncomfortably. He turns red when he realizes Mrs. Eberst not only knows what the "p" word is, but will say it out loud. "Look at me, Jon." He does until I repeat the "p" word and instantly looks down again at his feet. "A penis is a normal body part. All boys have them. Most boys love to talk about them. I understand that. I am a mother of a son." I sense he is beginning to relax, so I continue. "You need to remember that the word penis . . . " I watch as his body shudders. ". . . is for boy conversations. You need to be mindful that there are girls in the room and having a conversation that involves the word 'penis' should not be used in their company." I emphasize the word "penis" because I like watching him squirm.

"Okay. Am I in trouble?" he asks, looking at me out of the corner of his eye.

"No, as long as you stop using the word 'penis' in the library." He walks away, both relieved and mortified. His friend looks at him, then he looks at me. Knowing it is his turn to chat with the librarian, he sheepishly comes to my desk. I put my hand on his shoulder and say, "So, my friend, what inappropriate word are you using today? Please tell me it isn't PENIS." He cringes. Then in a tone much like Mike Brady talking to Greg on the *Brady Bunch*, I continue. "A penis is a normal body part. All boys have them. Most boys like to talk about them . . ."

6

Adventures When the Light Bulb Turns On

I love it when something clicks in a child's brain. Sometimes it's a concept they have been working hard to understand for a very long time. Sometimes it's a thought they've never had before. You can see it in their faces and hear it in their voices. Something just makes sense, and they can't wait to tell you about it.

Before school begins one morning, Chris runs into the library with a book in hand. She is so excited, she is talking a hundred miles an hour.

"Mrs. E., I was reading this book last night when I had this great thought. Did you know when you see the title of a book, by the end of the book, you find out why the author used that title? Isn't it brilliant?"

She gives me a high five and runs off to class. I can't help but smile and think that it is brilliant, indeed.

For me, though, what is truly brilliant is when a light bulb comes on for a child. The connection isn't always academic. There are times when they connect something to what they already know and build on that knowledge. When Ava left this note on my desk after earning a spot as a **Student Library Curator**, the connection she made was personal:

> Dear Mrs. Eberst,
>
> Yes! Yes! Yes! I am very happy that I made it for being a library curator. I worked my very hardest on my project. I wanted it to be all professional if you know what I mean. I was super confident and now I made it. It came to me that if I work hard and believe in myself I can do whatever I want to do in the future.
>
> Thank you, Ava

As delighted as I am when a light comes on for a student like Ava, who suddenly understands the value of an event in her life, I am equally excited when a light bulb goes on and a student gets my sarcastic sense of humor. Many times, I have to clarify my sarcasm by following up with, "I'm kidding!" Then a student will laugh or shake his head with amazement, showing me he "gets it." Whenever a child makes those important connections, it's always an adventure—no matter when or where a light bulb pops on.

Exploring the Telephone Booth

At the entrance of the library is a telephone booth. It is part of the Library Museum collection that gives students a chance to explore the "Pre-Cell Phone" era. The students are fascinated by the phone booth, and I am transported back to the days of my youth.

On this day, Jackie, a kindergartner, is excited to explore. She picks up the receiver and studies it. Appearing confused, she opens the door and asks, "How do you text?"

The Chuck Taylor Rule

I wear Chuck Taylor Converse shoes every day and have done so since becoming a librarian. The habit started when we wore black high-top Chuck Taylors as part of our costumes at Dirty Jack's Theatre in Wyoming. My Converse collection has grown over the years. Many are on display in the library. The variety of colors and designs fascinates the students, not just because they are now popular, but because many of the students wear the same size I do. For years, I have shopped in the children's department for shoes and gloves. It's a challenge to find dress shoes in a size 3 Youth that look adult. Most have sparkling pink bows or Dora the Explorer on the top. When it comes to Chuck Taylors, though, there's never a question about age or taste. My collection is vast, and every student is envious. I tell my students if they catch me at school without my Chucks, they win a prize.

One day, I ask a class of first graders who can tell me about my Chuck Taylor rule. A very excited young man raises his hand and says, "If we steal your Chuck Taylors and you don't catch us, then we win a prize." This is not *quite* what I say, but there is some truth in his statement.

Descendants

Pamela is a studious third grader interested in history. I tell her stories about people in Ohio history that are on my family tree. This interests her, and she goes home to learn about her family tree. She comes back to the library looking for research materials.

"Do you have a book on descendants?" she asks. I'm not sure if she wants the series from the fantasy fiction section so I ask, "*Descendants*, the series?"

"No," she explains, "I'm looking for a book on old dead people in my family."

"Old dead people in your family would be your ancestors," I say. "Your children will be your descendants." She lets me know she doesn't have any children.

"Someday, I hope you will."

"Then I would be an ancestor."

"Yes, that's true. Do you know what country your ancestors are from?"

"The country of Oregon," she says.

"I have ancestors from the Country and the State of Oregon, too," I tell her. Pamela gets very excited about this, suggesting maybe we might be related since we both have family in Oregon.

"We might be," I say. "We can do some research and find out."

I can see Pamela's brain working when she looks at me and asks if ancestors can be old alive people. "I suppose they could," I tell her.

"Then *you* could be my ancestor," she says.

Samwise Gamgee Has a Mother?

One of Caleb's favorite library activities is to look through the box of 45s. He thinks vinyl is the greatest invention ever, and after listening to a record, wants to know if you turn it over, will it play backward? He tells me once that he bought vinyl at the store and that one of the records was a group called the Rolling Stones. "I hear they're pretty good," he says. I tell him that I'd heard that too, then ask him if he knows how old the Rolling Stones are.

"Like 70 or something," he says. Connor, who is Caleb's partner in music exploration, overhears the conversation and tells me he thinks it's pretty cool that a group of grandpas got together and started a band. All I can say is bless Grandpa Mick.

The boys often spend extra time in the library searching for something new to put on the vintage record player. One day Caleb pulls a 45 of Patty Duke singing the theme song to her 1965 movie *Billie*.

"Who is Patty Duke?" they ask. For fun, I tell them she's Samwise Gamgee's mother.

"Samwise Gamgee has a mother?" they ask in disbelief.

"These must be the songs she sings in *Lord of the Rings*!" Caleb says enthusiastically.

She is Vintage

Part of the Library Museum experience is learning the vocabulary that goes with our collection of vintage technology. The first word we learn is "vintage." Melissa, a kindergartner, loves the word and is excited when she discovers that it's the same as saying "old."

In December, the kindergartners are overjoyed when they look down at my feet and see my Christmas Converse High Tops. These shoes are covered in fuzzy red candy cane stripes. Of course, they all want to touch them, so from my reading chair, I hold up my leg and let each child feel my shoe. As 25 five-year-olds gather around my raised leg, I say, "Everyone who wants to touch them needs to do it. I can't hold my leg up forever!"

Melissa, who always takes charge, shouts for everyone to hurry up and touch the shoe. "Mrs. Eberst can't hold her leg up forever! She is vintage."

Speaking Wyoming

We have a large ESL population in our building, where many students grow up speaking one language at school and another at home. Maria assumes that everyone lives this way, including me.

"I lived in Mexico before I came to Ohio. Where did you live?" she asks. I tell her that I lived on the other side of the country in the state of Wyoming. Maria is very excited about this information and asks, "Can you still speak Wyoming?"

"Yes, I can."

"Say something in Wyoming!" she asks excitedly.

I clear my throat, think for a moment and say, "Howdy, thar, little lady. Git up on that thar harse and go fer a ride. Giddy up. Whoa, thar fella." Maria looks at me for a moment and tells me that I sound like a cowboy.

"Wyoming is the Cowboy State," I say.

Very excited, she asks me if I can teach her how to speak Wyoming.

"Yup!" I reply.

You Read Your Brother's Journal?

Jacob earned a journal in the school reading competition. I overhear him as he announces to his friends, "You should see what my brother writes in *his* journal!" As he keeps talking to his friends, I hear them whisper and then giggle with looks of shock on their faces. Then I ask Jacob if he really reads his older brother's diary. Without hesitation he replies, "Yes."

"Does your brother know you're reading his journal?"

"No!" he says adamantly. "Do you think I'm crazy?"

I grab my cell phone and pull up his mother's number, speaking out loud as I text: "Your son has announced to the class today that he is secretly reading his brother's journal. Perhaps a chat is in order."

"Go, ahead," he dares me. "It's just a joke."

"Are you sure?" I ask.

"Sure," he says bravely. "I'm not scared."

I pretend to hit the send button. He bursts into tears.

"If you think it's just a joke, then why are you so upset?"

"I don't really read my brother's journal."

So I ask him again, "Then why are you so upset?"

Jacob doesn't say a word. He tells me that he really doesn't read his journal, but he does read his texts.

"You read your brother's texts?"

Jacob's head falls down in shame. He tells me that his brother is going to kill him. I put my hand on his shoulder and ask if he has learned anything from this.

"Yes, I've learned I shouldn't snoop in my brother's things, but if I do, I shouldn't tell anyone about it!"

Do You Speak Spanish?

There are three reasons a student usually doesn't pass an online Accelerated Reader test. One, they didn't read the book. Two, the book was too hard. Three, they chose the wrong test. When a student tells me they are having trouble taking a test, I go right to those three reasons.

Dana is frustrated when he tells me, "I'm trying to take an AR test, and I don't understand the questions."

"Did you read the book?" I ask.

"Yes."

"Is it in your range?"

"Yes," he says. "I just don't understand the questions." I look at the computer and see that he selected the Spanish version of the test. I am feeling a bit ornery, thinking that this could be fun and a good way to make my point. I ask if it would be helpful if I read the questions to him.

Sounding relieved he says, "Yes."

I don't speak Spanish, but I am fairly good at accents, so I knew I can pull this off. (I offer my apologies to those who are fluent in Spanish.) Clearing my throat, I read, "Question one: El Cinco de Mayo si uno mongo taco loco?" Dana stares at me. "Which answer do you choose? A, B, C or D?" I ask. He continues to stare with a blank expression.

"Did you read the book?" I ask.

"Yes," he says, sounding tense.

"You're sure the book is in your reading level?"

"Yes."

"Let's try another question. Si Si grande uno taco muncho el yum?"

Dana shakes his head and tells me he doesn't understand, so I ask him again if he is sure he read the book. "Yes," he says, growing more frustrated.

"Are you sure the book is on your reading level?" I ask again.

"I already told you that. It *is* my reading level," he says, a little louder than he intended.

"Let me ask you this." Then I pause. "You don't speak Spanish, do you?"

"No."

"Then why did you choose the Spanish version of the test?" By now he is completely frustrated and confused. "I don't know," he says.

"That, my friend, is not a good answer," I tell him. "There is no right or wrong answer to that question. Only *you* know why you selected this quiz."

Knowing I won't accept "I don't know" as an answer to another question, Dana says, "The picture next to the quiz is the same picture on the cover of my book."

"Did you read the title of the quiz?" I ask.

"No, I just looked at the picture."

I tell him that next time he should read the title before taking the quiz. This title reads, "Junie B. Jones y el autobus tonto y apestoso."

Dana smiles and says, "That's Spanish, so the quiz is in *Spanish?*"

"Yes, it is," I say.

Finally getting it, he says he picked the wrong test. I tell him he did.

"You were joking with me when you read the questions, weren't you, Mrs. Eberst?" I can see the light bulb turn on over his head when he speaks.

"Yes, Dana, I am."

He explains that he doesn't speak Spanish, and I tell him I already know that.

"You don't speak Spanish either, do you, Mrs. Eberst?"

"Why do you think that?" I ask him with a smile.

"Because there's nothing about a taco in the story." I tell him *that* is an excellent observation.

"Do you understand you need to read the title before you select the quiz?"

"Yes."

"What?" I ask. He says yes again.

"Not yes. Say 'si,'" and tell him I'm giving him a lesson from Spanish 101.

"You're funny, Mrs. Eberst."

"Thank you. I will cancel the test so you can take the right one."

"Thank you," he says, relieved to be able to take the test over.

"Say 'gracias.'"

He says gracias and goes on to pass the English version with flying colors.

I Know Where You Live

I tell students who forget to return what they borrow that I have been known to show up at their house to collect missing library books: "I know where you live," I tell them.

During a school levy season, another teacher and I hit the neighborhoods to talk to residents about the importance of voting "yes." We knock on the door of one of my students who is never late returning her library books. When Jett answers the door, she sees me standing there and looks startled, almost in shock. Before I can ask if her mother is home, Jett runs up the stairs, leaving us standing at the open door. She isn't gone a minute when she runs back down the stairs with a book in her outstretched hand.

Out of breath and with her eyes wide open, Jett hands me the book and says, "Here's my library book!"

For the rest of the year, she tells her classmates that when Mrs. Eberst says she will show up at their house to collect library books, she's not kidding.

It's in the Bible

Jennifer Ward wrote a wonderful read-a-loud entitled, *There is a Coyote Who Swallowed a Flea*. First graders love to hear this book read over and over. Sitting in front in the reading corner, Carrie lights up as she leads the rest of the class in calling out a line from the book: "Yippee Yo Ki yee!"

I keep reading aloud, "He swallowed the bird to catch the snake. He swallowed the snake to catch the lizard. He swallowed the lizard to . . . " until Carrie shouts out in the middle of the story, "That's in the Bible!"

"What is?" I ask.

"The part where he swallowed the bird to catch the snake."

I tell her that I have read the Bible, and I don't remember that part. She goes on to explain that it's in the Book of Generous: "Adam and Eve met the snake, and God had to stop the snake from bothering Adam and Eve, so he sent the bird to swallow the snake."

"Well then," I tell her, "I need to go home and read the book of Generous again. I can't believe I missed that part."

Carrie continues her biblical explanation: "He sent the snake to swallow Adam and Eve."

I'm curious, so I ask, "Why did he send the snake to swallow Adam and Eve?" She looks at me wondering why I would even have to ask such an obvious question.

"Because they ate the apple," she says.

Anita, who is sitting next to Carrie, chimes in with a sigh, "I love Bible stories!"

Do You Have a Handicap Sticker?

I hear sounds of struggle as I look up and see two first graders trying to drag a crate of books down the stairs and into the library. Each student checks out between three and four books a week. For a class of 25 students, this is a substantial number of books for two students who are assigned to return them on their library day. I hear the commotion at first, and as I look up from my desk, I see George and Jim trying to maneuver the crate down the three steps to the library.

"You know you can use the ramp," I tell them. "It's much easier to roll the crate down the ramp than to try to carry all of those books down the stairs."

George, who is not only environmentally conscious, but also mindful of the needs of others, points out that this is a ramp for the handicapped.

"By the looks of things, you have a handicap trying to get all those books into the library," I tell him.

Sternly, George instructs me about the reason the ramp is located in the library in the first place. "We don't use handicap things if we are not handicapped. You have to have a card that says you can use the ramp, like the one that lets my grandma park in a handicapped spot."

I listen and agree with him, but I add, "That's true, except the ramp going into the library is there to help all of us if we need it. When you try to bring back a crate full of all those books, you need the help of the ramp."

"It's for handicapped people!" he insists.

I don't want George or Jim to fall down the stairs, hurt themselves, or scatter books all over, so I offer my assistance. "Can I give you a handicapped pass to return the books down the ramp?" Before George can object, Jim shouts, "Yes!"

Then I take a sticky note and write in big letters:

OFFICIAL TEMPORARY
HANDICAP STICKER:

GOOD FOR GETTING CRATES OF BOOKS
INTO THE LIBRARY BY USING THE RAMP.

EXPIRATION:
WHEN THE BOOKS ARE ON MY DESK.

I walk the note to them, and George eyes me suspiciously. He tells me it isn't a real sticker and that there would be a $500.00 fine if they get caught. In that moment, I hear a crash and Jim, covered in sweat, looks up at me with library books scattered at his feet. Reaching out, he takes the temporary sticker from my hand and gives his disgruntled classmate a look that tells George not to say a word.

"I'll take it!" he says and starts picking up the books off the floor.

Flexible People

When speaking with a first grader, it's always a good idea to remember that you are speaking with a first grader. I forget that rule the day Laurie asks if I have a book on flexible people. Thinking of our school's core values I ask, "Do you mean people who work well with others? People who adapt to change?"

Laurie looks at me confused and repeats her request. "You know, flexible people."

I am a little slow and still uncertain what she's looking for. "Can you give me an example of what you mean?"

Laurie spreads her legs wide and bends over. Then she sticks her bottom out and lifts her chin while wrapping her arm around her head and turning her face up. Smiling while she strains to speak, She repeats, "You know, flexible people."

I still don't get it. "A contortionist?" I ask.

"I don't know what that means," she says, still straining to speak while bent over and twisting. "I want a book on flexible people."

It finally dawns on my what she is asking, so I bend over into the Downward Dog pose, look up at her and strain to speak myself. "Yoga?" I barely get the words out.

"Yes," Laurie says, looking up at me while still upside down. "Flexible people." If anyone walked by the library at that moment, they would have had no idea what was going on. Both Laurie and I are bent over, bottoms in the air, heads turned and having a conversation. She quickly stands up to get her book on yoga. It appears that I am not one of the flexible people because with Laurie's help, it takes me a minute to ease my way up from Downward Dog and guide her to the books on flexible people.

Don't I Know It, Sister!

Joyce is my Kindergarten Employee of the Week. She takes her job very seriously. She always asks for the student's library card and then scans the student's book. Joyce is an above-and-beyond employee, often commenting on how nice a student looks in the photo on his library card. Or she might hold up a book, and before scanning the barcode, tell a kindergarten patron, "I'm sure this is a book you will enjoy."

Her customer service skills are impeccable. After scanning 25 library cards and 50 books, Joyce puts her head down on my desk and sighs. "It is hard work being a librarian."

All I can say is, "Don't I know it, Sister!"

Technology Expert

Wendell comes to me one day with his laptop because he is having problems getting on our blended learning program. I just left a class where I couldn't fix a CHROME book, even though a student in the class told me I was the smartest person in the school. Determined to regain my "smartest person" status (which I had just lost with a third grader), I take Wendell's problem laptop from him. He watches me intently as I open and close files and programs. I have no idea what's wrong or how to fix it.

"Oh, yes, I see the problem," I say, adjusting my glasses and pressing random keys on the keyboard. "It looks like the master data file is not reading gigabyte driver 107. This means your transporter beam won't connect to I Ready Math. Until we have this fixed, it will never make the Kessel Run in less than 12 parsecs."

"I believed you until you said that last part," he says, taking back his laptop. "I'll go find someone else to help me."

As Wendell walks away, I give him the Mr. Spock Live Long and Prosper Signal, saying, "But Obi-Wan Kenobi, I'm your only hope!"

Wendell leaves the library without turning around to say goodbye. Apparently, my status as the smartest person in the building just took a nosedive.

7

Adventures in Innocence

Many children today are exposed to an early education about the realities of life far sooner than I was as a child. Though many children now see movies or TV shows that never played during my waking hours as a kid, or they sing lyrics with adult themes only insinuated in the sixties, children aren't as worldly as they often think they are or want to be. Some believe in Santa, while others show how grown up they are by proclaiming Santa doesn't exist. Then there are children who don't believe in Santa but won't say it out loud, just in case he might show up with presents on Christmas Eve.

Almost every day I'm asked by concerned six-year-olds if the picture on my desk of King Kong grabbing my husband and I at the Hollywood Wax Museum is real. When a first grader checks out a book on dinosaurs and tells me that dinosaurs make his heart sing, I'm delighted by such innocence. And my heart melts when a struggling reader looks at me and explains that she is a better reader when she has her sparkly shoes on.

Usually, I find that fourth graders want to be teenagers and teenagers want to be adults. But all children need the experiences of being a kid before they grow older. They need to see life through innocent eyes, so they can grow up knowing and keeping that perspective. The older you get, the more you long for an innocent perspective. Pablo Picasso says, "It takes a very long time to be young."

I am inspired by the innocent honesty of children. Their pure hearts and expressions lift my spirit and make me smile. The often naïve perspective of a child can put me in the place I need to be to reach students both academically and personally. Every day I have the opportunity to see the world through a child's eyes, and that view has always made me a better librarian and teacher.

I Am Waving

After the bus drops a group of students off in the morning, the driver motions me to come over. When I get on the bus, a lone first grader in tears stands by the driver.

"I'm not sure what to say to this child," he says. "I got a call from another driver that our friend here flipped him off when his bus passed ours."

Of all the students in the building, Steve is the last one I would ever expect this from. He is the definition of pure innocence with a face from a Gerber ad, complete with sweet round cheeks. He always wears a plaid collared shirt tucked into his khaki pants, which are held up high above his waist by a brown leather belt. I look down at Steve's tear-stained face and ask him, "Why?"

He starts to cry, asking me if he's in trouble because he was just waving to the other bus. I ask him to show me how he waved to the other bus. Standing in front of me, Steve flips me the bird.

"Steve, my friend, what you did is not waving. Did another student show you how to wave like that?" I ask.

"No," he says, trying to catch his breath. "My mom did."

"Your mom taught you to wave like that?" I'm not sure if he's protecting another student from getting into trouble, or maybe I just don't know his mom as well as I thought I did.

He goes on to explain that a car going fast passed his mom while she was driving. She must have known the person because she waved at the man in the car like that.

I smile at the driver, and he smiles back. We both understand Steve's mother.

I tell Steve I want him to go home and talk to his mom about what happened this morning. I try to explain that sometimes adults wave at people like that, but kids should never wave like that. "It's an adult thing," I say.

He gets himself together and asks again if he is in trouble. I tell him, "No, but remember, I want you to use all of your fingers when you are waving from now on."

Your Birthday Suit

Kindergartners have the best responses when we discuss stories. Audrey Wood's King Bidgood's *in the Bathtub* always inspires interesting results.

"How many of you play with toys in the bathtub like King Bidgood?" I ask. A great deal of giggles erupt and hands raise in answer to my question.

"How many of you eat lunch in the bathtub like King Bidgood? This time there are fewer giggles and fewer hands raised.

"How many of you go fishing in the bathtub like King Bidgood?" This time there are no hands raised and several groans of "yuck."

"How many of you dance in the bathtub like King Bidgood?" This time there are no hands raised. Then the kindergartners throw themselves on the floor in a fit of laughter, and then one concerned, "But you'd be naked?"

"How many of you have taken a bath in your birthday suit?" There is louder laughter; only one student admits to taking a bath in his birthday suit.

"I take a bath in my birthday suit," I say.

Wide-eyed kindergartners can't believe their ears. Mike asks who would take a bath in their birthday suit. "It would be ruined," he says.

Kelly smiles sweetly and tells me that she is going to go home and tell her mother that Mrs. Eberst takes a bath in her birthday suit!

I Found This on the Bus

The buses that come to the elementary school pick up and drop off high school students first. We never know what students are going to leave on the bus. Lynne hands me a note when she get to school and tells me she found it on the seat she was sitting in. The note is written inside the drawing of a lovely red heart in penmanship that would have made my fifth-grade teacher Harriett Parrot proud. This signed note reads: "I love you, and I will let you kiss me and do whatever else you want to do to me anytime you want to do it."

"Did you read it?" I ask, fanning myself from the heat that suddenly rushes to my head flushing my cheeks.

"I don't read that good and can't read fancy letters. It must be mushy cause it has a heart," says Lynne.

"Yes. It is mushy," I tell her.

That's the day I decide I'm going to stop driving my car to school and start riding the high school bus.

I'll Tell My Dad You
Are Thinking of Him

On occasion, I have had students try to set me up with their grandfathers, telling me it would be nice to have me as a member of the family. I thank them and tell them that Mr. Eberst doesn't let me date. Sometimes their matchmaking is obvious. Other times it takes me by surprise.

After checking out her books, Angie tells me that when she gets home, she is going to tell her dad that I say hello. I didn't think anything of it and tell her that would be great. The next day when she comes into the library, I think she wants to exchange her books, but instead, she stops in to tell me that her father isn't feeling well.

"I will tell my dad that you hope he feels better soon," says Angie.

"I didn't know he was sick," I say. "I hope he feels better." She smiles and tells me that she will be sure to tell him I want him to get better.

On the following day, I see her in the hall, and she stops to tell me that she told her dad that I am thinking about him. I think to myself, "That's an odd comment," but since I'm oblivious to her intentions, I tell her it's very nice of her.

The next day is the Invention Convention. As I walk around to student exhibits, Angie walks up to me, takes my hand, and whispers with a grin that her dad is here. She pulls me over to her dad, holding my hand in one of hers and her father's hand in the other. Joyfully looking at her father, Angie says, "Look Dad!

It's Mrs. Eberst." She then turns to me and with the same joyful gaze says, "Look Mrs. Eberst! It's my dad." Dad looks a little uncomfortable.

Then it quickly dawns on me that Angie is matchmaking. I let go of her hand, smile, and tell them both to enjoy the convention. Mr. Eberst is flexible when it comes to a lot of things, but dating a student's father is not one of them.

The Tooth Fairy

I am always touched when children share what is in their heart about what they believe. After the Virginia Tech shooting several years ago, our principal tells the students that it's important that they let their friends and family know how much they mean to them. After her announcement, I watch children hugging each other and even see a few tears as children express genuine feelings.

Then Harrison quietly makes his way to my desk. Tearfully, he whispers that there is something he has wanted to tell for a long time. Looking at me through his tears, he says, "Mrs. Eberst, Heavenly Father loves you no matter what." Although Harrison is grown up now, I will always remember his expression of love.

Many years after that day, students still share their heartfelt beliefs, just as Harrison did with me that day. For example, while they look at their library books together, I overhear Ben tell Jeanie, "I don't believe in the Tooth Fairy." With a look of concern, Jeanie asks him if he gets money under his pillow when he loses a tooth. Ben tells her he does.

"The Tooth Fairy doesn't care if you believe," Jeannie says sweetly.

"I don't believe in Santa Claus either," says Ben. Jeannie tells him that Santa is going to bring him presents anyway.

"Do you believe in God?" asks Jeannie.

"No," says Ben.

"He loves you anyway," she whispers.

Are You Wearing Lipstick?

Kindergartners notice everything. They have opinions about everything, and they aren't afraid to share them.

"Mrs. Eberst, are you wearing lipstick?" asks Jan.

"Yes, I am. Do you like it?"

"You look weird, but nice," she says.

"Thank you, I think," I say, smiling at her.

She looks at me with concern, studying my mouth. "You know, Mrs. Eberst, you shouldn't wear lipstick."

"Why not?"

"Lipstick is for kissing people, and library teachers don't kiss people."

Excuse Me, Say That Again

Paul is a student who does exactly what he's told. He follows every rule and makes sure I know he is following every rule. Not only that, he makes sure I know who isn't following the library rules. For example, I have paint sticks that I use as shelf markers to help students while they're exploring the shelves for books. The sticks help them remember where to put the book back on the shelf.

These are the rules that go along with the sticks:

1. Sticks are not toys.
2. Sticks are not to be used to sword fight.
3. You NEVER, above all else, WHACK anyone with a stick.

One afternoon when everyone is finished checking out books and busy reading around the library, an obedient Paul comes to me in a panic. His hands are shaking as he speaks. He looks disgusted and concerned, telling me that Charlie is whacking off in the back of the library. I'm not sure what I hear, so I ask him to say it again.

Paul leans in and looks at me as he emphasizes each word, shouting, "Charlie is whacking off in the back of the library!" I instantly go to the standard librarian line, putting my finger to my lips: "Shhh. Indoor voices. We are in the library." I've never actually uttered those words as a librarian, but today, my Librarian Training 101 is all I can think to draw on.

Calmly, I tell Paul to get his book, sit down and read. "I will take care of this," I assure him. Casually wandering around the library smiling at students, I comment at random on their choice of books until I find Charlie. He is lying on the floor on his stomach, reading his library book and tapping his head with a library stick. I exhale. Then, smiling at Charlie, I walk away thinking to myself, "Whack away, Charlie. Whack away!"

Can I Tell You Something?

I have worked very hard to communicate with my students. They are comfortable telling me things because I tell them things, and we listen to each other. They think they know my deepest secrets, like my first name or where I live. They vow never to share such secrets with another human being. Secrets. Information they proudly tell others they know but refuse to share. After all, someone gave them this information with trust and a pinkie promise. Sometimes children tell me more than I want to know (and certainly more than their parents want them to tell me).

Dean lives with a single mother and three siblings. He has talked to me about his parents' divorce before, so it isn't surprising when he asks if he can tell me something.

"Of course, you can. What's up?" I ask.

Without hesitation Dean says, "My mom has a penis in her drawer."

"I see," I say, not sure if he is telling me this to see how I will react, or if he is just sharing some general family information. "You know, you really should not get into things that don't belong to you," I tell him.

His eyes light up. "It shakes when you pick it up! It's cool," he says.

"Wow, that is cool," I tell him, sharing his genuine enthusiasm for this discovery. "Dean," I say. "You really need to stay out of your mom's dresser drawer unless you ask her first."

Dean smiles and while running back to class tells me, "Okay! I'll ask when I get home."

Best Friend Advice

Renee is a kindergartner who is always dressed in cute dresses with matching bows in her long wavy hair. I, on the other hand, wear what is comfortable and am lucky each day to have the same colored shoes on. There is a day when I realize I am wearing one black sock and one blue, which is a step up, considering the summer I was working at the Board office and drove half way to work before I noticed I didn't have my skirt on at all. As I got ready for work that morning, I tootled around without my skirt on, so it wouldn't wrinkle. I'm glad I had time that morning to turn my car around and go home to put on my skirt before walking into the Board office and noticing something was missing.

On this school day, I do remember to put on a little makeup. Renee watches with interest as I touch up my lipstick. "Why are you putting on lipstick?" she asks. The answer is easy. I tell her that my best friend Janet Benedict told me that you are never fully dressed without your lipstick.

Offering more advice, Rene kindly adds, "You are never fully dressed if you are naked either."

They Sound Kinda Silly

The first record that I play in the Library Museum is *The Chipmunks Sing the Beatles*. Ava asks me if I like the Beatles. I tell her yes, that they were among the most talented musicians of all time. She listens intently to each song. After hearing "I Want to Hold Your Hand," Ava says, "I think they sound kinda silly."

I apologize to Paul McCartney and Ringo Starr as I didn't explain for Ava the important difference between the Fab Four and the Chipmunks singing Beatle hits.

Will You Come Over to My House Tonight?

I am always being invited to student birthday parties and other events. My first year as a librarian, a kindergartner finds out that I live in his neighborhood and shows up on my family's doorstep one night at dinnertime. Looking down when he answers the door, my husband sees a round-faced little guy asking if Mrs. Eberst can come out and play. Carl politely tells him that I am having dinner and can't come out right now.

Another student, Scott, sees me in the hall and asks, "Will you come over to my house tonight?" I explain that I can't come over tonight. He tells that if I change my mind he will be home. "I'm not allowed to open the door when people come over, but if my parents are in the shower together and you come to the door, then I will answer it."

I thank him for inviting me over but warn, "Scott, sweetie. If your parents can't come to the door, do not open it for anyone. Not even me."

"Not even you?" he asks, thinking that doesn't make sense.

"Not even me!" I say.

"Okay," he says, "Maybe you should call first."

That Is the Worst Thing I've Ever Heard

I am often taken back by the experiences of some of my young students. The older I get, the more I see how the world has changed. Our kids are exposed to and experience things that never crossed our minds when we were their age. The most shocking experience for me was when I was in high school and met Lester. He was older and wiser than my 16 sheltered years, but I fell hard for him. We were both in the cast of a summer theatre production. One night before the show, he took me out to dinner and told me that he could not return the affections I had for him since he was gay. My sheltered response was, "I'm so happy too!" That was the day I learned there was more than one meaning to the word "gay." Today, even with all that my young friends are exposed to, they are still just kids, and their perceptions are that of kids, too.

Every library class I read to kids, and on this day, I read a story about two children who are fighting over a ball. The ball bounced out of the window so high that it shattered the moon into a million pieces. "They should go to jail!" Rocky shouts. My students know if they have a connection to something in the story, they can share during reading time. Several hands shoot up.

"My dad went to jail once."

"My brother was thrown in jail because he got caught with a girl."

"My uncle is in jail because he beat up my dad at my grandma's funeral."

My head is spinning as, all at once, students are raising their hands and shouting out their jail stories. I don't know what to think. With these connections, it's one student who causes the others to gasp in disbelief. Lorel speaks slowly. His voice is almost a whisper. We all lean in to listen. There is something in his voice, something in the expression on his face that causes the entire class to hold our breath. I can't quite tell if he is going to share something so horrible that I will have to rush to the guidance counselor for help or that what he tells us will be something so amazing that along with his classmates, I will forever look at him in awe.

Lorel whispers. "My brother went to jail because during the President's talk, he dropped his pants and showed his bare bottom to the President of the United States."

The class is silent, except for a small gasp. Teri puts her hand over her mouth, and all their little wide eyes are on me. "His bare bottom? That is bad. Really bad," she says. The class nods in agreement.

Rocky, who started this conversation when he said the characters in the story should go to jail, looks down at the floor. Shaking his head, he says, "That is the worst thing I have ever heard."

For Generations to Come

It's always a bit of a surprise when I find out that a student's mother is in one of my classes when she was in elementary school. Many times, I will recognize the name but not the face. But it's when a student tells me that I had their grandmother that I'm taken aback. Truth is, I didn't have their grandmother. Really, I didn't!

Kerry held her first chapter book close. "This is so wonderful, Mrs. Eberst. Thank you for letting me check out this book. This story has been handed down from generations in my family."

"Really?" I ask, looking at the book.

"Don't you remember that my mother checked it out and read it when she was a little girl? My grandmother read it when she was a little girl, too. Don't you remember? Now it's my turn. Generation after generation, we have checked out books from your library."

I look at the book that was published in 2016. "Thank you, Kerry. I'm glad I have been here for your family all these years!" I say.

Hopefully, she will love it and share it for generations to come.

Librarian Day

Bob is visibly struggling when his teacher asks what is wrong. He tells her that he is trying to make a Librarian Day card and is having trouble. When she asks him what is the problem, he says, "I don't know how to draw her wrinkles."

Where Have You Been?

Bobby is missing his library books for several weeks. One day, he is sure he never checked it out. The next day, he is telling me something exciting about what he read from that same book he said he's never seen. I can't get mad at him because he loves coming to the library. If he couldn't check out any books, he would sit on the floor and look at all the books he's going to check out once he finds the book he is sure he never checked out in the first place.

After making my rounds to visit students, I walk down the hall toward the library when an exasperated Bobby says, "Where have you been? I've been walking all over the school looking for you. I went to the library, and you weren't there." I tell him I had to see a student, so I was in the first-grade wing. "You are supposed to be in the library," he scolds me. "I went to every room in the building, looking for you. I found this book at Kiddie Academy. It is on the floor. Who checked it out?"

"I don't know, Bobby. I will take it back to the library and check it in." He tells me that he gave it to me because he is responsible. He makes it very clear that he found the book and turned it in and that made him responsible.

"You could have just left it on my desk," I say. "I would have found it. You don't have to walk all over the school looking for me. I don't want you to be late for class."

Holding up a tardy pass, he says, "It's okay because I have this!" He thinks that is his license to run around the building looking for me without getting in trouble. I tell him the pass had 8:45 written on it, and it is now 9:00. I turn him around and tell him to go to class. As he walks down the hall, he shouts, "Are you proud of me? I found a book on the floor, and I brought it back. I am responsible!"

When I get back to the library, I check the book in. The name of the student who checked it out is my tardy, responsible first grader, Bobby.

Adventures in Relationships

I grew up on Nelson Drive in a small Wyoming town. The road winds around the base of the mountains and dead ends at Mr. May's farm. Walking down Nelson Drive gave me my first sense of community. If I had a bad day at school or made a mistake, the word spread long before I got to my house. I would walk around the corner toward the final stretch home, and Mrs. Byrne would scold me from her front yard. Across the street, Mrs. Foltz would have a few words of her own. I didn't dare look up the hill because surely Mrs. Long or Mrs. Mower would look disappointed too. Then Mrs. Livingston would peer through her curtains without a smile, and Mr. Heinbough, who owned the junkyard across the street from my house, would take pleasure in announcing, "Man, are you in trouble now!"

Likewise, if I had a great day or accomplished something grand, I could count on Mrs. Byrne to shout from her yard, "Well done!" Mrs. Foltz would give me a "thumbs up," and without concern, I could look up the hill to see Mrs. Long and Mrs. Foltz both waving with a smile on their faces. Mr. Heinbough, still sporting that grumpy look, would give me a slight smile and tell me he was so proud of me. Then, if I wanted, he'd tell me I could come over and explore the junkyard—a place he usually chased us kids from. That junkyard exploration alone was the best reward for any accomplishment.

I learned a great deal about relationships from the people in my neighborhood. Being in school is much like Nelson Drive. Relationships are developed as children play together, learn, and have fun. School is a time for students to make mistakes and know they will not be judged by teachers, administrators, or school librarians. Children flourish when they're supported and learn how to fix mistakes. This is a time to celebrate their successes, whether academic or personal. In elementary school, a cheer for landing an assignment in the Principal's Exemplar Gallery is equal to celebrating a child's first lost tooth.

Once, six-year-old Kenny told me, "I really like it when I show you something, and you say, 'Wow!'" Hearing Kenny's gratitude reinforces what I know: the relationship of confidence and trust that I and other educators build with students becomes the foundation for the relationships they will develop throughout their lives. When children interact with adults and can feel comfortable expressing themselves freely, laughter results. From experience, I've learned that humor is the perfect tool for building successful, meaningful relationships with students.

More Like One of Us

Toby has thick glasses and his hair is always out of place. Today is no different when he says, "We like you better than the other teachers."

"Why is that?" I ask curiously.

"Because. You're more like one of us."

"Thanks," I say, as I wipe my runny nose on the sleeve of my shirt.

New Glasses?

I try to do the unexpected each time a class arrives. I act nonchalant about it. At first, students come into class, see my hat or costume, and start being disruptive. After a few months, though, students act like what I wear is nothing out of the ordinary. My Groucho Marx glasses (complete with a big nose, bushy eyebrows, and a mustache) was this week's disruption.

As Griff checks out his library books, I ask him, "Do my new glasses make my nose look big?"

"Yes, and hairy," he says.

"Do you think these eyebrows are a good look for me?"

He raises his own eyebrows and doesn't say a word. Leah is behind him and joins the conversation, saying, "I think you look pretty."

Griff turns around and looks at her, saying, "Are you kidding? Really?" to which she answers, "Yes, she looks pretty."

"Thanks, I think I look pretty too!" I say. Griff grabs his library books and turns back to me, giving me the same look he gave Leah.

"You people are weird," he says, shaking his head as he walks away.

Allergy Table

Every once in a while, I sit down at a table in the cafeteria and join students for lunch. This is always a treat for me and a surprise for the students. They act like teachers don't do things kids do. If they see me in a store or at a restaurant, they can't believe I'm there and want to know why I'm not at school. It's common knowledge among elementary students that teachers live in their classrooms.

"What are you doing?" Aiden asks suspiciously.

"Joining you for lunch. Can I sit here?" I ask. The boys look at each other and smile. Will wants to know what I have that I'm willing to trade for the sandwich his mother made while Aiden offers me a bite of his cookie.

With a mischievous grin, Luke tells me that I can't sit here. When I ask why, he points to the sign: "No nuts allowed."

Boys Can Be So Mean

First-grade girls Liz, Leah, and Kate run up to me as soon as they get off the bus to tell me that a boy is picking on them. Leah tells me he's a third-grade boy. Then she says, "He's being mean to us!"

"What is he doing?" I ask, concerned.

"He smiles at us," Leah says.

"And tells us we're pretty," adds Kate.

"And that someday he is going to marry us!" says Liz with a disgusted look on her face.

I look at the three traumatized little girls and tell them not to worry. "I understand how you feel," I say. "Boys can be so mean sometimes."

Then I send them off to class, thinking about how glad I am that my husband Carl was that mean to me 30 years ago.

This Is How You Become the Teacher's Favorite Student

To raise money for the math program, the high school hosts a 5K on March 14. This 5K day is better known in the world of education as Pi Day. It has been a very long time since I have participated in a 5K. I have no expectations of grandeur. When it came to athletics, the truth is I don't expect anything at all, other than making it across the finish line without needing to call the emergency squad. So I sign myself up alongside our staff, who are mostly younger and more athletic than I am.

When I get to the race, however, my little competitive spark kicks in. I'm suddenly determined that no one is going to beat the short, stocky redhead wearing khaki shorts and a Pi Day T-shirt. I am making great time as my fellow redheaded friend Audrey, a first grader, grabs my hand, telling me we should run across the finish line hand in hand. I agree. Through the last stretch, Audrey kicks it into full first-grade power, dragging me to a breathless victory.

My Pi Day 5K trophy sits in a place of honor on the circulation desk.

One day, a student sees the trophy, picks it up, and reads the inscription: "First Place Age Group 60 and Over."

"You actually finished a 5K, Mrs. Eberst?" Joe asks in surprise.

"Yes, I did," I say with pride. "And you can see by the trophy that not only did I finish, but I won!"

"It says for the 60-year-olds?"

"I'm not 60," I say. "I'm not even 58, yet." Then I tell him the story about how they gave the trophy to me because everyone else in my group was 15 years younger, and that my time was almost as fast and theirs, and that there were no other older people in the race.

"So, it's a gift," Joe says, matter of fact. "A mercy trophy."

"Something like that," I say.

Charisse, who is next in line to check out her books, overhears the conversation and says, "I can't believe you are 57 years old!"

I asked her how old she thinks I am.

"35," she says.

"I love you, Charisse," I say.

Then she smiles and turns to Joe, who is still holding my mercy trophy. "That," she says, "is how you become the teacher's favorite student."

"It worked," I say, smiling at Charisse. "You are my favorite student."

I'm Getting Two Presents for Christmas

Landon and I are friends the minute he walks into the library to visit his new school. He is a kindergartner. He looks shy at first glance, but after a second look, I notice a spark of mischief in his eyes and a bit of an evil grin on his cherubic face. Surely, we are kindred spirits.

One day at the end of library he comes up to my desk and innocently announces that he is getting two presents this year for Christmas. "I'm getting one from Santa and one from you." He turns around to walk away, then looks back at me over his shoulder and grins.

"Don't forget to wrap it," he says.

I Don't Like Her

Matt is a little socially awkward and has a hard time relating to most students. He slowly comes to me with a downtrodden demeanor. Sadly, he says, "No one will read with me. No one likes me. No one will be my friend."

"I will read with you. I like you. I will be your friend," I tell him gently.

"You're too old to be my friend!" he says. Overhearing this, Madison, with her long blonde hair and pixie face, ever so sweetly says, "I will read with you. I like you." She takes his hand to guide him toward a table. Matt hesitates. As he's being dragged away by his new friend, he looks back at me over his shoulder and with a panicked expression, mouths the words: "Help me! I don't like her!"

I'm Writing a Book

Ted, a kindergartner, is excited to share the news that he is writing a book.

I tell him that is brilliant. "I'm writing a book too," I say. "I'm almost finished with it. What is your book about?" I ask.

His face grows serious. Then he leans in to make sure he isn't going to be overheard by others in the room. "Death, bones coming to life. Scary stuff," he says. "I can't bring it to school because my dad said it would be too hard for people. What are you writing about?"

"My job. My students. Life. The silly things kids do in the library. Funny stuff," I say.

Ted looks at me for a minute and then asks, "Are you going to write about what I just told you?"

"May I?" I ask.

"Sure," he says.

"Are you going to write about me?" I ask. Once again, Ted leans in close, not wanting to be overheard by others. Then, quite seriously, he says, "No. I only write about death and bones coming to life. Scary stuff. It would be too hard for you. Someday I might write something about you."

"Thanks, Ted. I'm going to write about you today." I hope mentioning death, bones coming to life, and scary stuff won't be too much for my readers. Ted will be pleased.

Imaginary Friend

I am focused on my computer, which is not responding to what I need it to do, so I don't see a student standing at my desk. He waits patiently before interrupting, wanting me to look up. When I don't look up but continue to work, David, being ever so polite says, "Excuse me, Mrs. E. Do you always talk to your computer?"

Apparently, I am talking to the computer while working. I become concerned about what I might have been overheard saying to the uncooperative technology. I was raised in a bilingual household where we spoke English and profanity, so I'm not sure which language I have been mumbling to the computer screen. I look up, see no signs in his expression that I'm speaking any language other than my appropriate mother tongue and casually reply, "Yes. Don't you?"

"Not to my computer," he says. "But I talk to my imaginary friend."

That catches my attention. I look up from the screen and ask him if his imaginary friend has a name.

"Moojoski," says David. "He is half elephant and half dog."

"Does he talk back to you?" I ask.

"Yes. Does the computer talk back to you?"

I look at the screen, sure that the flashing message "file not found" is morphing into "Danger Will Robinson!" and forcefully hit the escape key. I tell David that my computer does, indeed, talk back. "It talks back all the time!" Then he looks at me with a peaceful expression and says, "I'm glad your computer is your imaginary friend."

Looking Over the Kingdom

Each week I post the top readers in the library. To reach the place where I put their names, I must stand on my desk. Students are in and out of the library all the time and have gotten used to seeing me doing what they think is strange. Nothing surprises Aiden.

"What are you doing up there?" he asks.

I turn and face the library. Raising both hands above my head, I announce in a booming voice, "I am the Librarian! I climb high above the room, so I can look over and admire my kingdom."

"You can be really strange sometimes," he says, and bends down to the floor.

When I see this, I continue my royal rant. "Thank you, my loyal patron. As you bow down to me, I recognize that you are indeed a patron of distinction! Rise, speak your request!"

He looks around to see if I'm really talking to him. "I am tying my shoe," he says.

Looking straight at him, I bellow, "Be gone! I cast you out of my presence." Aiden shrugs his shoulder like it's no big deal. "Fine. Can I check out my books first?"

"Sure, buddy," I say, holding out my hand for his assistance. "As long as you help me down from my desk."

Luke, I Am Your Librarian

Every May 4th, Star Wars Day, I wear my Darth Vader mask. Most of the time I forget I have it on. Lucas eyes me suspiciously, walking up to my desk to check out his books.

"Don't say it, Mrs. Eberst. I've heard it before," says Lucas.

"Heard what?"

"Luke, I am your father," he says, but not in a very good Vader imitation.

"I'm not going to say it," I tell him.

"Good," he says, "I'm sick of everyone saying it each time they say my name." He checks out his library books, and as he walks toward the door, I call to him in my best Darth Vader voice, "Luke. I am your Librarian."

I Will Never Do That Again

Gretchen, a third grader, knows my first name, so she thinks that we have a connection that I don't have with any other student. Because of that, she believes she can ask me anything, and I will answer.

"Is there anything that you've done in your life that you would never do again?" asks Gretchen. How do I answer that question for a third grader? I think for a minute while having a flashback to my twenties. I don't find anything in those files I can safely share with her, so I reach back farther into my past, a long time ago, in a galaxy far, far away when I am in elementary school.

"Yes," I say seriously.

She leans in closer so as not to miss a word of my confession. I speak slowly, looking around the room. She looks around the room too, both of us making sure this experience, once buried deep in my past, is only known by the two of us.

I tell her that I can never watch the movie *Bambi* or read the book *Old Yeller* ever again, no matter what, because I cried for days. Gretchen looks disappointed. I know she is looking for something more interesting and juicy about my past. She is unimpressed with the exploits of my youth but immediately goes to the bookshelves and picks out a copy of *Old Yeller*.

Say You're Sorry

Two tired kindergartners have a spat. No matter what, they are not going to let this go. I call them both to me and say to Casey, who started the argument, "Look Daryl in the eyes and say, 'I'm sorry.'"

Casey is missing her two front teeth, looks at her friend, and says, "Say I'm thorry."

Daryl looks right at her and tells her, "No, I didn't do anything. You did!"

"Casey, my sweet girl, you need to say I'm sorry to Daryl."

With her hands on her hips, she tells Daryl to "Say I'm thorry." Daryl shouts back that he isn't sorry. I finally figure out the communication breakdown.

"Casey, listen carefully to what I'm saying. Say," I pause, "I'm sorry." Then I pause again, pointing to Daryl, "to him."

Casey starts to tear up and says to me that I told her to say I'm sorry and that she already told Daryl to say I'm sorry.

I rephrase my request: "Apologize to him."

Casey looks at Daryl, wipes her tears and says, "I'm thorry." Daryl smiles, hugging his friend and telling her it's okay. They walk off hand in hand, leaving me tired and confused.

There Are Days I Wish I Were You

Second graders are busy putting away items for the Exploration Stations in the Library. Melody is overseeing what needs to be done, giving orders to everyone, and instructing them about where they should put the telephones and cameras. She looks a bit stressed as she runs from table to table, growing agitated when her classmates will not listen to her.

When the work is complete, Melody, with sweat on her brow and flushed cheeks, says, "There are days, Mrs. Eberst, when I wish I were you." I ask why. She goes on to change her mind, telling me that, in fact, she is already like me.

"How are you like me?" I ask.

"Well, I'm crazy, and I like to clean up after myself."

We Are Here for You

Summit Living Library Museum is a student-run library where every year students fill out an application, interview, and receive a job offer to work in the library or a rejection letter. Those chosen to sign a contract get a job description. Those not chosen shed tears. Student librarians run the circulation desk, learn to put books back on the shelf, and give up one recess a week to help when needed. Their contract also reads, "All other duties so assigned." I added this line to their contract because if my contract reads like that, so should theirs.

These jobs are open for kindergarten through fourth grade. Some apply because they think it will be fun, not knowing how much work is involved. Others think working the circulation desk is a badge of honor. Some students figure it's a good way to get out of recess, while others take it so seriously they will do anything to prove their commitment to me, their employer.

Ryan, a third grader, is willing to give up every recess if I let him, regardless of his weekly work schedule. He loves his job and takes it very seriously. After helping label new books at recess, he leaves to go to lunch. As he's leaving, he stops at the door, looks at me, and makes his dedication to his job very clear. "I am here for you, Mrs. Eberst. Whatever you need, I am here for you. Unless, of course you have pinkeye. Then I am not here for you."

Will You Marry Me?

Mrs. Cicak, one of our reading teachers, came to me and shared that while working with Lisa, a kindergartner, she is told that Lisa loves coming to the library and that she really loves Mrs. Eberst. Lisa says, "I wish Mrs. Eberst were my mother, so I could kiss her on the lips." Mrs. Cicak tells her that she should be sure and tell Mrs. Eberst, this since it would make her very happy. After getting this report, I can't wait for Lisa to come to the library that afternoon.

Lisa is the first one in the library. With a big smile on her face, she runs up to me, throwing her arms around me to confess, "Mrs. Eberst, I love you. I want to kiss you on the lips. Will you marry me?"

That is not how I thought this was going to go. I wasn't expecting a proposal. Kneeling down, I look at her smiling face. "Thank you so much. I love you, too, but Mr. Eberst won't let me marry anyone else. How about a hug?"

She throws her arms around me and gives me the biggest hug I have ever gotten.

The Power of Pokémon

I buy a large box of Pokémon cards as incentives. Once I start giving them away, I learn their true power. For example, they can silence a loud class of students in an instant. One day, I give directions to a class to read silently. Then one student who is dutifully reading finds a Pokémon card slipped into the pages of his book. "It looks like you need a bookmark," I smile. Suddenly, the entire class is reading or pretending to read, including Jimmy, who is reading intently from a book he's holding upside down.

Pokémon cards can also put a smile on the face of a kid who thinks that when an adult speaks to him, it is only to scold him. I call Jason over before he gets on the bus. Looking defensive, he asks me, "What did I do? I didn't do it!"

"What did you do? You came to school today and that makes me happy. You always have a spring in your step and you have a great smile." Handing him a Pokémon card, I say, "I have something for you because you are so great!" Jason grins all the way to the bus.

Pokémon cards can lift the chin of a boy who is always looking down. "Come here, Eric. I need to talk to you," I say. "Have I told you how much I love having you in the library?" He shakes his head no. "Well, I do. And it's about time you know it, too. I think you are a wonderful person, and I really like you. Have a great weekend." I put my hand on Eric's shoulder and hand him a card. He throws his arms around me and gets in line for the bus. I turn as I walk toward the building to see him smiling and waving at me.

I think to myself, "I'm going to like getting rid of all these Pokémon cards!"

What Do You Do All Day?

My morning is busy and flies by, so I grab a quick bite of lunch at my desk. I am rarely in the library without students wandering in and out, so they are used to finding me behind my desk wiping my mouth with a napkin. My student workers on duty that day have not yet shown up for work.

"Why are you eating your lunch at your desk?" Gareth asks me. I tell him that I am very busy today, and I want to grab something to eat before my next class, which will be here shortly. He turns and sees the student librarians who are giving up their recess enter the room. "You don't do much all day, do you?" he asks me suspiciously. I take immediate offense. "Excuse me?" I say. Looking over at the students busy putting books away, he explains that I hire all those kids to work for me: "They scan the books that are checked out and put them back on the shelf when they're returned. What else is there to do?" he asks in a judgmental tone.

I look at him, put my finger up to my lips, and say, "Shhhh. I don't want anyone else to hear this. All these student workers are a part of my plan. The more students I hire to work in the library, the less work I have to do all day." I lift up my potato chip bag, offering him a bribe, telling him not to tell anyone. Taking the bribe, Gareth says, "OK. It will be our secret." I tell him how much I appreciate him and that it's nice to have someone in my confidence. Then I open my container of hummus and offer him some. He shakes his head no, and says, "No worries. I got your back."

"Thanks Man. Glad to hear it," I say and offer him a cookie.

The Three-Second Rule

While I am on lunch duty, a horrified girl points to the boy sitting next to her and tells me that he just ate something off the floor.

"Really?" I ask.

He tells me that it is his food; it fell on the floor, so he picked it up and ate it. He then reminds me of the three-second rule.

"It's so dirty. Don't eat off the floor."

I ask him what he dropped. When he tells me it's chocolate, I tell him the three-second rule does not apply. I go on to explain that I probably would have picked it up and eaten it too.

"When it comes to chocolate, there is no three-second rule. There's a three-day rule."

We are pleased. Without having to say a word, we clearly understand each other while the girl who told on him is disgusted with us both. As I walked away, I notice a Tootsie Roll under the table that had been there since Monday. I smile and think to myself, "Mmmmm, yummy."

9

Adventures in Discovering You Matter

A few years ago, I returned to Wyoming and walked down Nelson Drive. I closed my eyes when a familiar mountain breeze blew across my face. That breeze transported me back in time. I stood on the corner and watched Mrs. Byrne busy in her yard, wishing I could walk over and thank her for everything she had ever done for me. Then I looked over at the Foltz house, wishing I could go inside and have a slice of bread and butter sprinkled with sugar that Mrs. Foltz always served when we played. I looked up the hill searching for Mrs. Long and Mrs. Mower and waved. Looking down the long road, which isn't as long as I remembered, I wished I could go see Mr. Heinbough and his junkyard, both of which are gone, so I could thank him for letting us use the old car hood as a sled.

As I stood on the corner, I realized that I wasn't just a kid in the neighborhood. Standing there, I understood that I mattered to each person and they mattered to me. I also realized that in part, I am who I am today because everyone on Nelson Drive mattered.

Every elementary school should be every child's Nelson Drive. Years from now, when they return and walk down the halls of elementary school as they did as a child, they will remember their first day of kindergarten. They will remember a smiling teacher standing at the door to greet them. No doubt, they will be amazed at how small the building seems or how close to the ground the water fountain sits. I want their visit to their elementary school to overcome them with joy as mine did when I returned home. I want them to have fond memories of a teacher who spent time with them, a secretary who gave them a hug, or a librarian who made them laugh themselves to tears in the library.

I want their memories to be so vivid that they know school wasn't just a place where they learned to read and write, but that their little school was a place where they were once part of a community, a community that helped shape them. Most important, I want them to know that school was a place where they first discovered they truly mattered.

I've Waited a Long Time for This

I've waited a very long time for this. I met Jeremy a few years ago when he toured the school with his mother. He was angry. He never smiled. A year later, he became a student at Summit. He is still angry and never smiles. We struggle to reach him. Every day, we chip away at the shell he has built around himself. Once in a while, Jeremy will begin to soften, only to return the next day with his shell harder and more impenetrable than the day before.

After a rehearsal for our second-grade show, he makes it very clear he will not be there for the evening performance. Instead of being relieved, I give him a job as a prop man and tell him it's important. "I need you to be there." His eyes light up. "OK," he says. He comes to the show and does his job. The next day at school he thanks me for giving him the responsibility of the props.

He still gets angry. He still struggles to smile, but he's getting there. His hard shell is starting to peel away. One day he drops a note off to me and goes back to his class without saying a word. As I read the note, I have to step out of the library to compose myself before I can get back to my students.

Jeremy's note reads, "Dear Mrs. Eberst, thank you for being a great Librarian and thank you for always showing me the new books you get. You are the number one Librarian that I have ever met. Know that we all love you. You believe in yourself and you are so kind that I think all the kids love to see you. Just to say that I am very close to you and that you are the funniest teacher." He signs the letter with his name, followed by a big red heart.

I walk into Jeremy's classroom where he is working at his desk. Kneeling down, I tell him with tears in my eyes, "Thank you. I am so glad we're friends." He smiles at me and has a calm look on his face like I've never seen before. Then, very sweetly, he whispers, "You're welcome."

I've waited a very long time for this.

Fear Not, I Will Protect You

I admit I am not a fan of reptiles and rodents. I prefer big animals, like moose and elk. Because we live in Ohio, moose and elk aren't readily available and don't make very good class pets. For some reason, though, teachers think it's a good idea to have a gerbil, a mouse, a snake, or even a rat as a class pet. It is, however, common knowledge around the school that I do not welcome animals in the library.

Then one day Mrs. Cannon visits to announce that her class gerbil had somehow found its way out of its cage last night. She knows that before police, animal control, or the SWAT team are called, Mrs. Eberst must be informed of any rodent or reptile escape in the building. I need time, after all, to block off the entrance to the library and sit on top of my desk until the creature is captured and safely returned to its cage. Teachers like Mrs. Cannon know that students will learn new vocabulary words if I see a mouse or a rat hiding in my shoes or running across my feet. Finding dead crickets in the toes of my Converse is bad enough. If something alive is hiding in my reading corner, there will be, well . . . hell to pay.

On this day, I appreciate that Mrs. Cannon drops by to give me a heads-up. While she is trying to get me to come down off my desk, assuring me that the gerbil is friendly, a student walks in and hears the news of the deadly rodent that has put the entire building, especially the library and the school librarian, in jeopardy. I'm impressed that this student doesn't panic, but instead walks to my desk, stands with his legs wide, hands on hips, and chest puffed out. "Fear not," he bellows loudly. "I will protect you!"

Going to Heaven

Students are always asking me how old I am. Some are generous in their answers and some are not.

"Mrs. Eberst, how old are you?" Rita asks.

"How old do you think I am?"

"Are you about ready to go to Heaven?" she asks gently.

"Do you think I'm old enough that I'm about ready to go to heaven?" I ask.

"No" she says sweetly. "I think you are nice, so you will go to heaven."

Hat Tip

When students or staff members in our school deserve recognition for doing something wonderful, we give them a "hat tip" during our morning meeting. Our principal has the student or staff member stand, and we all tip our imaginary hat in the person's direction to honor him or her with praise and admiration. It's a great honor and the recipient's pride, regardless of age, lasts long into the day and is always remembered. The look on the faces of those who tip their hats is equal to the joy of the one receiving such recognition.

One day, two second-grade boys run into the library and give me a big hug. This is no ordinary quick hug. It is a long group hug. Then they smile, step back, take a low bow, and end with a hat tip.

I start to cry.

Then they trot off to class, quite pleased with themselves.

He Is Groovy

Konne has a smile on her face, and her eyes are sparkling when she gets off the bus. I have never seen her look so happy. I say good morning to her as she walks past me, obviously thinking about something wonderful.

"Good morning," she sighs. "I saw that boy who has hair that goes like this on his face." She smiles and brushes her hand across her forehead. "I don't think he saw me. I can't breathe."

"I know what you mean. When I was your age, I knew a boy named Bruce who had hair like that," I say, brushing my hand across my forehead. "Every time I saw him, my hands would get sweaty, and my heart would pound faster. He was groovy," I say, remembering my first real crush. We went to school together from elementary through high school, and each time I saw him over the years, he had the same effect on me.

Konne and I stand outside the door as other students hurry past us to start the school day. We both look off into the distance and sigh. She looks at me, understanding exactly what I am saying. "Have a good day, Mrs. Eberst," she says, floating into the building. I think to myself, "I'm very glad she knows what it is to have her heart all a flutter."

Hi, Busty!

Natalie, a first-grade librarian, looks up at me with a grin and says, "Hi, Busty!"

Not sure if I heard her correctly, I ask, "What?"

She smiles again and says, "I heard a fourth grader say you are her bust friend. You are my bust friend too." As I offer her a high five, she says again, "Hi, Busty!"

I Am Somebody

I arrive at school early to catch up on a few things when I pass a student in the hall. He is at school for morning tutoring before school begins. Having arrived several weeks ago, he is fairly new to the school.

"Excuse me," he asks. "Are you the principal?"

"No, Will, I'm the librarian."

"You aren't the principal?"

"No. I'm not the principal. I'm the librarian."

He looks at me with a quizzical expression. "You're the librarian?"

"Yes," I say. "I am the librarian."

"I knew you were somebody," he says, looking at me.

"Yes, Will, I am somebody."

"Ok, then, have a nice day," he says, walking away.

I Could Eat You Up

Dana is as wide as he is tall and has a grin to match. He loves showing his affections to the staff with great big bear hugs. At the end of each day, he runs out of the building like it's on fire. When you see Dana coming toward you with arms open wide, you know to brace yourself.

This day I'm on bus duty when he comes running. Before I can tell him to slow down, he has his arms around me. "Mrs. Eberst, I love you so much!" he says, squeezing tight.

"I love you, too, Dana."

"My grandma says she loves me so much she could just eat me up. Well, I could just eat you up!" Reaching around and grabbing my bottom with both hands, he holds on tight and begins to chomp across my chest like he is eating a piece of buttered corn on the cob. I grab his shoulders tightly, trying to keep my balance and composure while pushing him away. The firmer I push, the tighter he holds on.

"I love, love, love you!" he sings.

I desperately look over at my colleagues who are laughing hysterically with no intention of intervening. Then, as fast as Dana grabs me, he lets go and runs to his bus, turning around with a wave. "See you tomorrow!" he shouts.

I am speechless. Eyes wide, mouth open, and holding my arms across my chest, I am barely able to utter a goodbye.

A Beautifully Wrapped Package

Children are always generous when it comes to gift giving. They often bring in "favorite teacher" mugs, chocolate, or the coveted Starbucks gift cards. One day, Nancy proudly holds up a beautifully wrapped package in front of me and gently sets it on my desk. "This is for you," she says.

"Thank you, Nancy. But it isn't Christmas. It isn't my birthday. It isn't even the last day of school. What's the occasion?" I ask.

She tells me there's no special reason, but she just wanted to give this special gift to me. I get a little choked up at her gesture.

"This is so thoughtful and kind of you. May I open it?" I ask, trying to hold back my emotions.

"Yes," she beams, as she tells me how much she knows I will like it. I pick up the gift, shake it, smile, and slowly unwrap the box. Gently lifting the lid, I look inside.

"This is wonderful! You know just what to get me. I can't tell you how much I will treasure this gift. It is honestly the most thoughtful gift I have ever been given," I say. "Thank you so much."

Nancy is pleased with herself. She runs off to class saying, "You're welcome!"

So what was in the box? Nancy's overdue library books.

Determined to Find a Way

Every time Stan comes to the library, he won't look at me. He won't speak to me, and he makes it very clear when he pushes my hand away that he doesn't want to be touched. This is difficult for me, since I am one of those teachers always putting my arm around students or touching their shoulder when I speak to them. He doesn't always come to the library with his class, but when he does, he won't check out a book but will just sit on the floor in the reading corner. I am determined to find a way to reach him.

I get word that he likes Pokémon cards and that he needs an incentive since he's learning his boundaries as well as how to stay focused and connect with other students. I become his incentive. On Fridays, if Stan has a good week, he can come to the library and trade Pokémon cards with me. He always looks at the stack, picks out the ones he wants, and replaces them with the ones he is willing to part with, all without looking at me or saying a word.

After a few weeks, he runs up to me after arriving at school, puts his head on my shoulder for a minute, and without a word, runs to class. From that day on, he calls me by my name, and I find out he likes to draw, to play with my hand puppets, and to write stories on the electric typewriter in the Library Museum—all after he checks out his library books. Struggling to wait his turn, Stan often loses patience with me when I'm giving the lecture to students about missing library books. "You are wasting our time!" he says, not being disrespectful, but in his own way, telling me that he and his friends are ready to explore the library! I always answer, "Yes, Stan you are correct."

While giving the evil eye to the same students who are missing books each week, I support Stan's statement, saying, "Missing book lectures are a waste of time!" Which is my code phrase to Stan that he can now enjoy the library.

I'm Your Biggest Fan.

It is "Read Across Ohio" week, and I am asked to take our students on an adventure dressed as Miss Frizzle from *The Magic School Bus*. I wear a red dress covered with pictures of Ohio, a necklace of Buckeyes, and matching Buckeye shoes. My natural curly red hair sticks out in every direction and my own Lizzie the rubber lizard sits on my shoulder. As requested, I take the students on a pre-technology, use-your-imagination adventure, complete with a roller-coaster ride, actual water, and a tornado, all while sitting on a bus parked in the school parking lot.

Brittany, a wide-eyed kindergartner, asks if I am Mrs. Eberst. "No," I tell her. "I am Miss Frizzle. Mrs. Eberst is my twin sister." Her eyes fill with tears. Throwing her arms around me and between sobs, she cries, "I watch you every day. I am your biggest fan. I love you!"

On Behalf of Johnny Depp and Myself

At the end of each school year, the fourth graders fill out a survey for the yearbook. They share their favorite movie, TV show, singer, book, school lunch. The survey ends with their favorite actor and actress. On one survey, a child misspells "Johny Depp" as his favorite actor and "Mrs. Eberst" as his favorite actress. All I can say is, "On behalf of Johnny Depp and myself, I humbly accept this award."

The Perfect Gift

"I have something special for you," Cathy tells me. "I want to thank you for letting me check out library books. I saw this and thought you would like it." I thank her and take the folded paper from her. When I open it, I see the gift that all librarians hope for: a neatly clipped coupon for $1.00 off Ore Ida Tater Tots and Kraft Cheese.

"This is the perfect gift!" I tell her. "Every librarian needs tater tots and cheese!"

Marianna

One of my favorite teachers, Marianna Batson Augé, was also my friend. I loved her, and I know that she loved me. I loved her laughter. I loved how her eyes would light up when she talked about her children and grandchildren. I loved her stories. I loved her advice. I loved her friendship, and the day I got word that she had passed away was a trying one for me.

I was teary as I drove to work, thinking about the phone calls we shared over the years. She was a second mother. I thought about the many letters she wrote to me from Wyoming. I thought about the last time I saw her. A year ago, I walked into her room in the nursing home where she was struggling with Alzheimer's. Preparing me, Marianna's husband told me she might not remember who I was, but that didn't matter to me. I just wanted to be in her company again. I will never forget how her face lit up when she saw me. She even remembered details of conversations and letters that we shared. My picture was on the wall by her bed. I will never forget how I felt when she held me in her arms as we said goodbye for what would be the last time.

The day after I was told that Marianna has died, I was not sure how I would hold myself together when students came to the library. My class that day was kindergarten. After they checked out their books, I told them to be sure to take them home and have their mom and dad read to them. One little boy looked up at me and told me he doesn't have a mom. "She is dead. Jesus came in the night and didn't make her better."

I got down on my knees, so I could be face to face with Jordan. I tell him that I am sorry and that I believe his mom is always looking out for him. His eyes get wide as he says, "Really?" I told him that my friend Marianna died last night, and I believe that she is looking out for me. "I'm sure your mom and my friend Marianna are together in heaven looking down saying how happy they are that you and I are together in the library." Jordan smiles and shakes his head yes. I couldn't say any more because I knew I would burst into tears if I did.

After class, I had an appointment with a high school student who asked to be my intern. We met and chatted about her goals, including what she wants to accomplish over the year. I was impressed and knew she would be a good fit to become my intern. I apologized that I didn't remember her name. I wished I could use the excuse that I was a bit preoccupied for forgetting her name, but in truth, I'm well known for not remembering names.

"Marianna" she says.

I asked if I heard her correctly. "Marianna? Not Mary Ann?" She smiles and repeats her name: Marianna. It was a tough day, but Marianna got her internship, and I got confirmation that everything was going to be okay.

Not Much Difference Between the Two

Educators never know how deep their influence is to a student. Our reach is vast, and future careers are often chosen because of a student's connection to a particular teacher. Charlotte is a kindergartner whose mother shares with me that one day Charlotte came home and announced that when she grows up, she either wants to be Mrs. Eberst or the lady who rides elephants in the circus.

Not much difference between the two.

CONCLUSION

A Wonderful Life

Several years ago, I had the privilege of speaking to a group of fourth graders who were getting ready to move on to fifth grade. I have known this group of children since they were in kindergarten. Today they seem all grown up. Many will have children of their own. As I speak to them, I share that there are three things they need in life to be happy.

1. They need to love and be loved. Their parents have this covered, and someday they will meet a person who will make their heart flutter.

2. They need to have something to do. The job they have now is to be a student. Their job description is to be curious, to explore, to learn, and to make a difference.

3. They need to have something to look forward to. The possibilities are endless. Life is an adventure, not just to be dreamt of, but to be lived.

As I prepared for giving this talk, I went to the students ahead of time and asked them to write down what they dreamed of and what they wanted to accomplish. They gave me a variety of answers, with quite a few being "professional athlete" or "famous movie star." One young girl wrote that she wanted to be the First Lady, Vice-President, *and* President of the United States—not such an unreachable goal today as it was when she first wrote it.

One student wrote words that will never leave me. In fact, her message drives much of how I work with children every day: "Someday," she wrote, "I dream I will be a wonderful doctor or a really good hair-and-nail person. I dream that someday I will have a wonderful family, just like my mom and dad. I already have a wonderful family. What I dream most of all is I will grow up and have a wonderful life."

This is the purpose for which every educator I know has entered the world of teaching. We are here to give our students experiences, opportunities, skills, new ideas, and lifelong relationships. We are here to plant seeds and nourish hopes and dreams that will open doors for our students to have a wonderful life. No one knows what life will bring. But what I have learned from other educators, and from the children and parents who have entered my classroom, and from my own personal experiences, is that what a life in education brings—with all its joys and sorrows; its failures and accomplishments; its tears, love, and laughter—is, indeed, wonderful.

About the Author

B orn and raised in Jackson Hole, Wyoming, Rhonda Willford Eberst spent ten summers performing at Dirty Jack's Wild West Theatre. Her extensive acting experience and her work with National Park Tours organizing vacations for summer visitors set the stage for a life of speaking and performing.

After falling in love and marrying her husband, Carl, Rhonda moved to Ohio in 1986. Soon, the Ohio State Buckeyes replaced her beloved Rocky Mountains, but she continues to feel passionate about both. Rhonda and her husband raised four children. She was a stay at home mother until her youngest daughter entered kindergarten. Then Rhonda began volunteering at her daughter's school and working as a substitute educator. Carl and Rhonda now have three grandchildren, five grand dogs, and one grand cat that lives in the barn.

Before becoming a full-time educator, Rhonda taught Travel and Tourism for two years at a Paraprofessional school in Columbus, Ohio. Then she found her true calling when she was hired as a librarian for Reynoldsburg City Schools. Rhonda has the ability to find funny in everything, which has served her well as an educator.

For the last twenty years, she has been laughing with and at children, all while turning hundreds of students on to reading. She is passionate about kids and believes that when children know they matter, they will thrive, regardless of their circumstances.

Rhonda currently works at Summit STEM Elementary School. She is an author, humorist, speaker and Director of the Summit STEM Living Library Museum where she plays for a living.

CPSIA information can be obtained
at www.ICGtesting.com
Printed in the USA
LVOW12s1129040518
575972LV00001B/91/P